Kids Learn!

Review Third Grade
Get Ready for Fourth Grade

Editor-in-Chief
Sharon Coan, M.S.Ed.

Editorial Manager
Gisela Lee, M.A.

Editors
Jenni Corcoran, M.A.Ed.
Maria Elvira Gallardo, M.A.
Wanda Kelly, M.A.
Kathy Knoblock, M.A Ed.
Jodene Smith, M.A.Ed.

Creative Director
Lee Aucoin

Imaging
Phil Garcia
Sandra Riley
Misty Shaw
Don Tran

Publisher
Rachelle Cracchiolo, M.S.Ed.

Teacher Created Materials
5301 Oceanus Drive
Huntington Beach, CA 92649
www.tcmpub.com
ISBN 978-1-4258-0118-2

Reprinted 2010

Table of Contents

Useful Ideas and Suggestions for Parents

Ideas y sugerencias útiles para padres

Things to Do at Home

To Practice Reading

- Cut out the comic section of the local paper. Have your child practice reading the comic strips. You may want to screen the comics for age-appropriate content and language.
- Make a list of the things you want your child to do each day (or week). Have your child read the list in order to know what to do. Provide an incentive if your child reads and follows the directions to complete all of the things on the list.
- Press the mute button on the television. TVs built in the last 15 years have closed-captioning in which what is being spoken is written at the bottom of the screen. Have your child read his or her favorite TV show.
- Have your child read the entertainment section of the newspaper in order to find something for the family to do over the weekend. There are often many free events available to the community each weekend. Have your child plan when to leave, where to go, and what to do once you are there.

To Practice Writing

- Have your child write a description of someone living in your house (or something in your house). Challenge him or her to write the description without using the person's name. Have him or her read the description to the rest of the family. Is the family able to guess who was written about based on the description?
- Cut out the headline of a newspaper article. Have your child write an article that matches the headline. The contents of the article can be invented.
- Encourage your child to write a fairy tale. Remind him or her that the fairy tale needs to have a beginning, middle, and end. Provide pencils, crayons or markers, and paper for your child to create a book once the fairy tale is finished. Have him or her read the book to a younger sibling or neighbor.
- Have your child write an invitation to a friend for a play date. The invitation should include the date, time, and location of the play date. Provide an envelope and stamp so your child can mail the invitation to his or her friend.

To Practice Math

- Let your child cut coupons out of the newspaper. Find out how much each item costs at the grocery store. Have your child calculate the new price of each item once the coupon has been discounted. Have your child figure out the new price of the item if the grocery store doubled the coupon discount.
- Have your child help you in the kitchen as you prepare a recipe. Your child can practice reading the recipe and measuring out the ingredients. If possible, half, double, or triple the recipe to provide additional measurement practice.
- Watch the news to find out the temperature each day. Have your child make a graph showing the temperature each day of the week. Ask questions such as: "Which day had the highest/lowest temperature?" "What was the difference between the highest and lowest temperature this week?" Create graphs for several weeks. Compare the temperatures over the period of a month.
- Have your child write and solve math problems using the scores from the sports section of the newspaper. He or she can compare scores of sports teams, compare scores of individual athletes, or find the difference in scores.

Cosas para hacer en casa

Para practicar la lectura

- Recorte la sección de historietas del periódico local. Pídale a su hijo o hija que practique leyendo las historietas. Es conveniente que usted lea la historieta primero para ver si el contenido es adecuado para la edad.
- Haga una lista de cosas que quiere que su hijo haga cada día (o semana). Pídale que lea la lista para saber qué tiene que hacer. Ofrezca un incentivo si el niño lee y sigue las instrucciones para completar todas las cosas de la lista.
- Oprima el botón "mute" del televisor. Los televisores de los últimos 15 años tienen subtitulado, donde lo que se dice aparece escrito en la parte inferior de la pantalla. Pídale a su hijo que lea sus programas de TV favoritos.
- Pídale a su hijo que lea la sección de espectáculos del periódico para encontrar algo que la familia pueda hacer el fin de semana. A menudo hay eventos gratuitos los fines de semana. Pídale a su hijo que planee cuándo salir, adónde ir y qué hacer cuando lleguen.

Para practicar la escritura

- Pídale a su hija o hijo que escriba una descripción de alguien que viva en su casa (o alguna cosa de su casa). Desafíelo a escribir una descripción sin usar el nombre de la persona. Pídale que lea la descripción al resto de la familia. ¿Pudo la familia adivinar de quién se trataba basado en la descripción?
- Recorte el titular de un artículo del periódico. Pídale a su hijo que escriba un artículo que concuerde con el titular. El contenido del artículo puede ser inventado.
- Anime a su hijo a escribir un cuento de hadas. Recuérdele que el cuento debe tener introducción, nudo y desenlace. Déle lápices, crayolas o marcadores y hojas para que haga un libro cuando el cuento esté terminado. Pídale que se lo lea a sus hermanos más pequeños o a un vecino.
- Pídale a su hijo que escriba una invitación a un amigo o amiga para venir a jugar. La invitación debe incluir la fecha, la hora y el lugar de la cita. Déle un sobre y una estampilla para que pueda enviar la invitación por correo.

Para practicar las matemáticas

- Deje que su hijo o hija recorte cupones del periódico. Averigüe cuánto cuesta cada artículo en la tienda. Pídale a su hijo que calcule el nuevo precio de cada artículo con el descuento del cupón. Pídale que calcule el nuevo precio del artículo si la tienda duplicara el descuento del cupón.
- Pídale a su hijo que le ayude en la cocina mientras prepara una receta. Su hijo puede practicar leyendo la receta y midiendo los ingredientes. De ser posible, divida en dos, duplique o triplique la receta para practicar más con las medidas.
- Miren las noticias para averiguar la temperatura todos los días. Pídale a su hijo que haga una gráfica donde muestre la temperatura cada día de la semana. Hágale preguntas como: "¿Qué día tuvimos la temperatura más alta/más baja?" "¿Cuál fue la diferencia entre la temperatura más alta y más baja de esta semana?" Hagan gráficas para varias semanas. Comparen la temperatura durante un mes.
- Pídale a su hijo que escriba y resuelva problemas de matemáticas usando los resultados de la sección de deportes del periódico. Su hijo puede comparar los resultados de los distintos equipos, comparar los resultados de atletas individuales o encontrar la diferencia entre las anotaciones.

Things to Do in the Community

To Practice Reading

- Make weekly trips to the local public library. Have your child check out books of interest to him or her. Explore a new section of the library each time you visit. Encourage your child to check out at least one book from the new section.
- Have your child read the return policy at a store in which you make a purchase. Stores' return policies are usually printed on signs behind the cash register or on the back of the receipt. Have your child summarize the policy for you and determine the date by which any returns or exchanges must be made.
- Provide your child with a map of your town or city. Have him or her practice reading it to determine where landmarks in your community are located.
- Have your child help you find food items in the grocery store by reading the signs above the aisles. Your child can also help you determine which brands to purchase by reading the labels to determine brands with healthier ingredients.

To Practice Writing

- Visit a store in your community that you may not usually frequent but may be of great interest to your child, such as a reptile pet shop, a costume store, or a flower shop. Have your child write about his or her experience and why the store was so unique compared to other stores you frequently visit.
- Provide your child with a small notebook and have him or her write directions as you travel to a location in the community, such as the grocery store or bank. When you get to each intersection, have him or her write down the name of the street and whether you turn right, left, or continue on the street. Have your child read the directions to you as you follow them the next time you visit that location.
- Have your child write down rules that he or she should follow when on playground equipment at the park. Encourage your child to list three rules for each piece of equipment, beginning with the most important. Have your child share the rules with a younger sibling or neighbor.
- Have your child write a review after seeing a movie. Describe the characters and plot of the movie so that someone who has not seen it will be able to understand more about it. Be sure to include whether or not others should see the movie.

To Practice Math

- Have your child figure out how many cars can fit in a parking lot. Encourage your child to count how many cars can park in one row and then multiply that number by the number of rows in the parking lot. This activity can be done in many other places, too.
- When ordering food at a fast food restaurant, have your child total his or her order. For example, have him or her determine the total cost of a hamburger, french fries, and soda. Allow him or her to pay for the bill and then practice counting the change to ensure it was correctly given.
- Have your child estimate how many people are in a room or store such as at a restaurant, bank, or grocery store. Encourage your child to count ten people and then use that as the basis to make his or her estimate. If time allows, have your child actually count the number of people and compare that to his or her estimate.
- Have your child determine the amount of time elapsed during a movie. Write down the beginning and ending times of a movie and have your child figure out the length of the movie. Pose additional problems such as, "What if there were two more previews that each last 5 minutes? How long would have we been in the theater?"

Cosas para hacer en la comunidad

Para practicar la lectura

- Hagan visitas semanales a la biblioteca pública local. Pídale a su hijo que saque libros que le interesen. En cada visita, exploren una sección nueva de la biblioteca. Anime a su hijo a sacar al menos un libro de la sección nueva.
- Pídale a su hijo que lea los carteles de la política de devoluciones de las tiendas donde haga compras. Esta política suele estar impresa en carteles detrás de la caja o en el reverso de los recibos. Pídale a su hijo que le resuma la política y determine hasta qué fecha pueden hacerse devoluciones o cambios.
- Déle a su hijo un mapa de su ciudad. Pídale que practique leyéndolo para determinar dónde se ubican puntos importantes de su comunidad.
- Pídale a su hijo que le ayude a encontrar alimentos en la tienda leyendo los carteles encima de los pasillos. Su hijo también le puede ayudar a decidir qué marcas comprar leyendo las etiquetas y eligiendo las marcas con los ingredientes más sanos.

Para practicar la escritura

- Visite una tienda de su comunidad a la que no suele ir, pero que pueda interesarle mucho a su hijo, como una tienda de mascotas donde vendan reptiles, una tienda de disfraces o una florería. Pídale a su hijo que escriba sobre esta experiencia y por qué la tienda era diferente en comparación con otras tiendas que visitan frecuentemente.
- Déle a su hijo una libreta pequeña y pídale que escriba instrucciones mientras van a un lugar de su comunidad, como la tienda o el banco. Cuando lleguen a cada esquina, pídale que escriba los nombres de las calles y si deben girar a la derecha, a la izquierda o seguir por la misma calle. Pídale a su hijo que le lea las instrucciones para seguirlas la próxima vez que vayan a ese lugar.
- Pídale a su hijo que escriba reglas que debe seguir cuando esté jugando en los juegos del parque. Anímelo a enumerar tres reglas para cada juego, empezando por la más importante. Pídale que las comparta con un hermano más pequeño o un vecino.
- Pídale a su hijo que escriba una reseña después de ver una película. Debe describir los personajes y el argumento para que alguien que no la haya visto pueda entenderla. Asegúrese de que incluya si piensa que los demás deben verla o no.

Para practicar las matemáticas

- Pídale a su hijo que calcule cuántos autos entran en un estacionamiento. Anímelo a contar cuántos autos pueden estacionarse en una fila, y multiplique ese número por la cantidad de filas del estacionamiento. Esta actividad también se puede hacer en muchos otros lugares.
- Al ordenar comida en un restaurante, pídale a su hijo que calcule el total de la orden. Por ejemplo, pídale que determine el costo total de una hamburguesa, papas fritas y refresco. Permítale pagar la cuenta y después practiquen contando el vuelto para asegurarse de que está bien dado.
- Pídale a su hijo que estime cuántas personas hay en una habitación o tienda, como por ejemplo un restaurante, banco o tienda de alimentos. Anímelo a contar diez personas y después usar eso como base para sus otras estimaciones. Si tiene suficiente tiempo, pídale que cuente de una en una la cantidad de personas y compare ese número con su estimación.
- Pídale a su hijo que determine la cantidad de tiempo que transcurrió durante una película. Escriba la hora de inicio y la hora de fin de una película y pídale que calcule la duración. Plantee problemas adicionales, como: "¿Y qué pasaría si hubiera dos preestrenos más de 5 minutos cada uno? ¿Cuánto tiempo habríamos estado en el cine?"

Introduction to Vacation Reading

The next page provides a list of recommended literature for children and adolescents in grades 3 and 4. The titles listed are recommendations for vacation reading for your child. The list includes both fiction and nonfiction books so that your child will experience a wide variety of types of reading similar to what he or she experiences in the classroom.

In each group of pages within this book, your child will be asked to select a book to read and to complete an activity related to that book. This list will provide some guidance in making those selections. These are only suggestions, however. If your child chooses other reading material, that is fine. Children will be more likely to read what they have chosen themselves.

Visits to your local library so your child can choose books to read will prove invaluable in helping your child maintain the gains in reading that have been made over the past year. Make sure your child chooses books that are at a reading level that is comfortable for him or her. If the books on this list seem too hard or too easy for your child, ask the librarian for guidance in choosing books that are leveled appropriately.

Most of all, make sure your child has chosen books that are interesting to him or her. Vacation reading should be fun!

Introducción a la lectura de las vacaciones

La siguiente página proporciona una lista de literatura recomendada para niños y adolescentes de 3° y 4° grado. Los títulos enumerados son sugerencias de lectura para su hijo durante las vacaciones. La lista comprende tanto libros de ficción como de no ficción para que su hijo o hija experimente con una amplia variedad de tipos de lectura, similar a la que se le ofrece en el salón de clase.

En cada juego de páginas de este libro, su hijo deberá seleccionar un libro para leer y completar una actividad relacionada. Esta lista sirve como guía para elegir una lectura, sin embargo, se trata sólo de sugerencias. Si su hijo prefiere otro material de lectura, está bien. Es más probable que los niños lean lo que han elegido por sí mismos.

Las visitas a la biblioteca local para que su hijo pueda elegir libros qué leer son una ayuda invaluable para ayudarlo a mantener los avances logrados durante el año anterior. Asegúrese de que su hijo elija libros con un nivel de lectura con el que se sienta cómodo. Si los libros de la lista resultan muy difíciles o muy fáciles para su hijo, pídale al bibliotecario que les ayude a elegir libros del nivel correcto.

Lo más importante, es asegurarse de que su hijo haya elegido libros que sean de su interés. ¡La lectura durante las vacaciones debe de ser divertida!

Suggested Vacation Reading

These books are recommended for students in grades 3 and 4. Most, if not all, of these books are available at your local library or bookstore.

Estos libros son recomendados para estudiantes de 3° y 4° grado. La mayoría de estos libros, si no es que todos, están disponibles en su biblioteca local o librería.

Grade 3

Author	Title
Cleary, Beverly	*The Mouse and the Motorcycle*
Dahl, Roald	*James and the Giant Peach*
Estes, Eleanor	*The Hundred Dresses*
Friedman, Ina R.	*How My Parents Learned to Eat*
Levine, Gail Carson	*Ella Enchanted*
Lowry, Lois	*All About Sam*
Miles, Miska	*Annie and the Old One*
Rockwell, Thomas	*How to Eat Fried Worms*
White, E.B.	*Stuart Little*

Grade 4

Author	Title
Babbitt, Natalie	*Tuck Everlasting*
Byars, Betsy Cromer	*The Summer of the Swans*
Cleary, Beverly	*Ramona and Her Father*
Cleary, Beverly	*Ramona the Pest*
Curtis, Christopher Paul	*Bud, Not Buddy*
DiCamillo, Kate	*Because of Winn-Dixie*
Fleischman, Sid	*Whipping Boy*
Gardiner, John Reynolds	*Stone Fox*
Juster, Norton	*The Phantom Tollbooth*
Konigsburg, E.L.	*From the Mixed-Up Files of Mrs. Basil E. Frankweiler*
L'Engle, Madeleine	*A Wrinkle in Time*
Patterson, Katherine	*Bridge to Terabithia*
Patterson, Katherine	*The Great Gilly Hopkins*
Raskin, Ellen	*The Westing Game*
Silverstein, Shel	*Where the Sidewalk Ends: The Poems and Drawings of Shel Silverstein*

Reading Log

Help your child complete this reading log to keep track of his or her vacation reading.

Ayude a su hijo a completar este registro de lectura para llevar la cuenta de su lectura durante las vacaciones.

Date	Title	Number of Pages	Author

Websites for Parents and Kids

- Fact Monster
  http://www.factmonster.com/
  Atlas, almanacs, dictionary, thesaurus, world, U.S., people, and more
- Edupuppy
  http://www.edupuppy.com/index.htm
  Large database of pre-screened sites appropriate for kids and their families
- Children's Book Council
  http://www.cbcbooks.org/
  Tips for reading to young children and reading activities
- Book Adventure
  http://www.bookadventure.com/
  Book quizzes for many of the books found on the California Reading List
- Read, Write, Think
  http://www.readwritethink.org/materials/in_the_bag/index.html
  Student materials that support literacy learning in the K–12 classroom
- Kidsource
  http://www.kidsource.com
  Activities for children from infancy to age 10
- Reading Rockets
  http://www.readingrockets.org/series.php
  Information, activities, and advice for parents
- ¡Colorín Colorado!
  http://www.colorincolorado.org/
  Information, activities, and advice for parents and educators of Spanish-speaking students
- Reading is Fundamental
  http://www.rif.org/parents/
  Ideas for parents to encourage reading at home
- Bookhive
  http://www.bookhive.org/
  Book reviews and recommendations
- Primary Computer Games
  http://www.primarygames.com/
  Educational computer games for elementary children
- Helping Your Child Learn Math
  http://www.ed.gov/pubs/parents/Math/index.html
  Math activities to do at home, at the grocery store, on the road, etc.
- Math Games
  http://www.mathplayground.com/index.html
  Math games for students in grades K–6
- Ask Dr. Math
  http://mathforum.org/dr.math/
  Question and answer service for math students and parents
- PBS Early Math
  http://www.pbs.org/parents/earlymath/grades_flash.html
  Math-based activities and developmental milestones for children from 6 to 9 years old
- Aunty Math
  http://www.dupagechildrensmuseum.org/aunty/
  Real-life problem solving challenges appropriate for grades K–5
- Cool Math for Kids
  http://www.coolmath4kids.com/
  Math games, puzzles, calculators, etc.
- Figure This! Math Challenges for Families
  http://www.figurethis.org/
  Math problems to challenge families
- A+ Math
  http://www.aplusmath.com/Flashcards/
  Math flash cards for addition, subtraction, multiplication, and division

Spanish Websites for Students and Parents
Sitios web en español para los estudiantes y los padres

- ***Mundo Latino***
  http://www.mundolatino.org/rinconcito
  Base de datos extensivo para personas que hablan español a nivel mundial con enlaces a todos los temas, de juegos educativos y revistas en la red.
- ***EduHound Español***
  http://www.eduhound.com/espanol/
  Base de datos al día de más de 30,000 enlaces educativos en todos los temas
- ***StoryPlace***
  http://www.storyplace.org/sp/storyplace.asp
  Lo último en la biblioteca digital de los niños. Explore estas páginas llenas de cuentos para niños, jóvenes y adultos.
- ***¡Colorín Colorado!***
  http://www.colorincolorado.org/
  Información, actividades y consejos para padres y maestros de estudiantes que hablan español

Reading Fluency

Reading fluency is the ability to read with accuracy and speed, as well as with proper expression.

Accuracy is the number of words that are read correctly. Accuracy develops as a result of many opportunities to practice reading with a considerable amount of success. Therefore, your child should read and reread text that contains mostly words he or she can read or decode easily. If your child misreads more than 1 out of every 10 words, the text is probably too difficult for him or her, even if assistance is provided.

Reading rate or speed is the rate at which a student can read a given text. Non-fluent readers will read slowly and deliberately, whereas fluent readers will read quickly and easily. One way to determine your child's reading rate is to calculate the number of words he or she can read correctly in one minute.

To determine your child's reading rate,

1. Select reading materials at the right level for your child.
2. Ask your child to read aloud for exactly one minute.
3. On a separate sheet of paper, make a note of any words your child misreads.
4. Count the total number of correct words your child reads in one minute.
5. The result is your child's reading rate or the number of words read correctly per minute (WPM).

The table shows the grade-level benchmarks for reading rate.

Reading Fluency Chart

Grade	Reading Rate
1st	60 wpm
2nd	90 wpm
3rd	115 wpm
4th	130 wpm
5th+	145 wpm

Fluidez en la lectura

La fluidez en la lectura es la habilidad de leer con precisión y velocidad, utilizando además la entonación correcta.

La precisión es la cantidad de palabras leídas correctamente. Se desarrolla como resultado de muchas oportunidades de práctica de lectura con un grado considerable de éxito. Por lo tanto, su hijo o hija debe leer una y otra vez aquellos textos que contengan principalmente palabras que puede leer o descifrar fácilmente. Si su hijo se equivoca más de 1 vez cada 10 palabras, posiblemente el texto sea demasiado difícil, incluso si se le brinda asistencia.

La velocidad de lectura es la velocidad con la cual el estudiante puede leer un texto dado. Los lectores que no tienen fluidez leerán de forma lenta y deliberada, mientras que los lectores con fluidez leerán rápidamente y fácilmente. Una manera de determinar la velocidad de lectura de su hijo es calcular la cantidad de palabras que lee correctamente en un minuto.

Para determinar la velocidad de lectura,

1. Seleccione material de lectura del nivel correcto para su hijo.
2. Pídale a su hijo que lea en voz alta exactamente por un minuto.
3. En una hoja aparte, anote cuantas palabras lee mal.
4. Cuente el total de palabras correctas que su hijo leyó en un minuto.
5. El resultado es la velocidad de lectura o la cantidad de palabras leídas correctamente por minuto (PPM).

La siguiente tabla muestra la velocidad de lectura esperada para cada grado.

Tabla de fluidez en la lectura

Grado	Velocidad de lectura
1°	60 ppm
2°	90 ppm
3°	115 ppm
4°	130 ppm
5°+	145 ppm

Strategies for Fluency Practice

Read Alouds

To read fluently, your child must first hear what fluent reading sounds like. One of the best ways for you to help your child become a more fluent reader is to read aloud to him or her often and with great expression. Carefully choose the books you read to your child. Make sure you select a wide variety of genres, including fiction, nonfiction, poetry, nursery rhymes, and folk and fairy tales. Also, read books that will spark your child's interests and draw him or her into the reading experience.

Model Reading

Have your child select a book on his or her reading level. First read aloud to your child, providing him or her with a model of fluent reading, while he or she follows along in the book. Then your child should read aloud the same book while you provide assistance and encouragement.

Choral Reading

Select a book on your child's reading level. Read aloud to your child and invite him or her to join in as he or she recognizes the words. Continue to read and reread the book, encouraging your child to read along with you. Your child should read the book with you several times. After the third or fourth reading, your child should be able to read the text independently.

Estrategias para practicar la fluidez

Lectura en voz alta

Para poder leer con fluidez, los niños deben antes escuchar cómo es una lectura fluida. Una de las mejores maneras en que puede ayudarles a leer con más fluidez es leer en voz alta a menudo y con gran entonación. Elija cuidadosamente los libros que lee a su hijo. Asegúrese de elegir una amplia variedad de géneros, donde se incluya la ficción, no ficción, poesía, versos infantiles, y cuentos folclóricos y de hadas. También lea libros que despierten el interés de su hijo y lo atraigan a la experiencia de la lectura.

Lectura modelo

Haga que su hijo elija un libro a su nivel de lectura. Primero léaselo en voz alta, a modo de modelo de lectura fluida, mientras su hijo le sigue en el libro. Después, su hijo debe leer en voz alta el mismo libro, con su ayuda y aliento.

Lectura al mismo tiempo

Elija un libro al nivel de lectura de su hijo. Léaselo en voz alta e invite a su hijo a unírsele a medida que reconoce las palabras. Continúe leyendo el libro una y otra vez, alentando a su hijo a leer con usted. Su hijo tendrá que leer el libro con usted varias veces. Después de la tercera o cuarta vez, su hijo debe poder leer el texto de manera independiente.

Glossary

A

alphabetical order: the arrangement of words according to the letters of the alphabet

angle: the space between two lines coming from a common point

area: the measurement of the space of a given surface

C

consonant: any letter that is not a vowel

contraction: a word formed by combining two words, some letters are left out and an apostrophe is used in their place

D

declarative sentence: a sentence that makes a statement

denominator: the number written below the line in a fraction; it refers to the number of equal parts

detail: information that tells more about the main idea

digit: any of the numbers 0–9

E

exclamatory sentence: a sentence that expresses strong feeling; usually followed by an exclamation point

F

fact: a statement that can be proven and that everyone accepts as true

fiction: stories written from the imagination; not true

fluency: the ability to recognize and read words quickly and accurately

H

homophone: words that sound the same but are spelled differently and have different meanings (for example, *ate* and *eight*)

I

imperative sentence: a sentence that gives a command

interrogative sentence: a sentence that asks a question

M

main idea: the main topic, usually of a piece of writing

N

narrative: one type of writing that gives the details of an experience or event

nonfiction: true accounts of an object, idea, or event in book or story form

numerator: the number written above the line in a fraction; it refers to the number of equal parts being referenced

O

opinion: one person's idea; everyone does not have to accept that it is correct

Glossary *(cont.)*

P

perimeter: the measure around the outside of a particular space

predicate: any part of a sentence that is not part of the subject, usually the verb, describing words. and clauses

proper noun: the specific name of a person, place, thing, or idea (for example, California)

R

root word: a word before prefixes or suffixes have been added to it (for example, the root of *jumping* is *jump*)

rounding: a way of working with numbers to make estimates (for example, numbers can be rounded to the nearest 10, 100, or 1,000)

S

subject: a noun or pronoun that tells who or what a sentence is about

synonym: words that have the same or almost the same meaning (for example, *bucket* and *pail*)

U

unit cost: the cost of one individual item

V

vowel: the letters *a, e, i, o, u,* and sometimes *w* and *y*

Glosario

A

ángulo: el espacio entre dos líneas que parten de un punto único

área: superficie comprendida dentro de un perímetro

C

consonante: cualquier letra que no sea una vocal

contracción: palabra formada por la combinación de dos palabras, en la que algunas letras se omiten; en inglés, se usa un apóstrofe en su lugar

costo unitario: el costo de un artículo individual

D

denominador: número que se escribe debajo de la línea de fracción; se refiere a la cantidad de partes iguales

detalle: da más información sobre la idea principal

dígito: cualquier número del 0 al 9

F

ficción: historias escritas desde la imaginación; no son verdaderas

fluidez: la capacidad de reconocer y leer las palabras rápidamente y con precisión

H

hecho: una afirmación que se puede comprobar y que todos aceptan como verdadera

homófono: palabras que suenan igual pero que se escriben distinto y tienen distinto significado (por ejemplo: *ate* y *eight* en inglés)

I

idea principal: el tema principal de un texto, por ejemplo, de un párrafo

N

narración: tipo de redacción que da detalles sobre una experiencia o acontecimiento

no ficción: relato de un evento o descripción de un objeto real en un libro o en forma de historia

numerador: número que se escribe arriba de la línea de fracción; se refiere a la cantidad de partes iguales a la que se hace referencia

O

opinión: lo que piensa una persona. No todos tienen que aceptar que sea correcta.

oración enunciativa: oración que hace una declaración

oración exclamativa: oración que expresa un sentimiento fuerte

oración imperativa: oración que da una orden

oración interrogativa: oración que hace una pregunta

orden alfabético: disposición de las palabras según las letras del abecedario

Glosario *(cont.)*

P

palabra raíz: una palabra antes de que se le agreguen prefijos o sufijos (por ejemplo, la raíz de *jumping* es *jump*)

perímetro: la medida alrededor del exterior de un espacio en particular

predicado: cualquier parte de una oración que no sea parte del sujeto, por lo general el verbo, palabras descriptivas y proposiciones

R

redondear: una manera de trabajar con números para hacer estimaciones (por ejemplo, los números se pueden redondear a la decena, centena o millar más cercano)

S

sinónimo: palabras que tienen el mismo o casi el mismo significado (por ejemplo, *cubo* y *balde*)

sujeto: sustantivo o pronombre que indica sobre qué o quién es la oración

sustantivo propio: el nombre específico de una persona, lugar, cosa o idea (por ejemplo, California)

V

vocal: las letras *a-e-i-o-u* y a veces en inglés *w* e *y*

Tips for Using This Book

This book has been designed to provide your child practice with skills and concepts while your child is on break from school. The book is divided into six weekly units. Each week has 10 pages of language arts and math practice. At the end of each week there is a challenge project for which your child may have to use several skills and concepts. Following are some tips for using this book with your child.

- Set aside a specific time of day to work on the book. This will establish consistency. An alternative is to look for times in your day or week that are less hectic and more conducive to practicing skills.
- Emphasize completing a couple of pages each time your child works in the book, rather than an entire week's worth of activity pages at one time. Completing several pages each day helps your child continually review and practice.
- Keep all practice sessions with your child positive and constructive. If the mood becomes tense, or you and your child get frustrated, set the book aside and look for another time for your child to practice.
- Help with instructions, if necessary. If your child is having difficulty understanding what to do, work some of the problems through with him or her.
- An answer key is provided on pages 97–100 at the back of this book. Once your child has completed the desired number of pages for the day, help your child check his or her work. If possible, take time to go back and correct any problems missed. Help your child learn from his or her mistakes.
- A completion certificate is provided at the end of each week. Once your child has completed the pages for a week, complete the certificate together. Filling out the certificate validates the importance of the work he or she has done, as well as shows a goal has been met.

Consejos para usar este libro

Este libro ha sido diseñado para que su hijo o hija practique destrezas y conceptos mientras está de vacaciones de la escuela. El libro está dividido en seis unidades semanales. Cada semana tiene 10 páginas para practicar artes del lenguaje y matemáticas. Al final de cada semana, hay un proyecto de desafío en el que su hijo puede usar diversas destrezas y conceptos. A continuación ofrecemos algunos consejos para usar este libro junto con su hijo.

- Dedique una hora del día en especial para trabajar con el libro. De esta forma establecerá regularidad. Una alternativa es buscar momentos del día o la semana que sean menos ajetreados y más propicios para practicar las destrezas.
- Insista en completar un par de páginas cada vez que su hijo trabaje en el libro en lugar de hacer al mismo tiempo las actividades para toda la semana. Completar varias páginas por día ayudará a su hijo a repasar y practicar continuamente.
- Haga que las sesiones de práctica con su hijo sean positivas y constructivas. Si el estado de ánimo se pone tenso, o si usted o su hijo se sienten frustrados, deje el libro y busque otro momento para que su hijo practique.
- Ayúdelo con las instrucciones si es necesario. Si su hijo tiene problemas para entender lo que debe hacer, trabaje con él en algunos de los problemas.
- En las páginas 97–100 del libro están las respuestas. Cuando su hijo haya completado la cantidad de páginas deseada para ese día, ayúdelo a corregir su trabajo. Si es posible, dedique un momento a volver atrás y corregir los problemas en que se equivocó. Ayude a su hijo a aprender de sus errores.
- Al final de cada semana se proporciona un certificado de terminación. Cuando su hijo haya completado las páginas de la semana, llenen el certificado juntos. Llenar el certificado da validez a la importancia del trabajo realizado y además muestra que se ha cumplido un objetivo.

Weekly Activities for Students

Actividades semanales para estudiantes

Beginning Sounds

How many different words can you make with each group of letters? Write the beginning consonants on the lines below each letter group to make new words.

¿Cuántas palabras distintas puedes formar con cada grupo de letras? Escribe las consonantes iniciales en los renglones debajo de cada grupo de letras para formar palabras nuevas.

___an	___ark	___eat
man		

___ame	___ear	___our

___ine	___ice	___up

Earth's Cycle of Seasons

Read the reading passage and then answer the questions below.

Lee el cuento y luego responde a las preguntas.

Earth's spinning causes a cycle of changing seasons. There are four seasons each year: spring, summer, autumn, and winter. The seasons are not the same everywhere at the same time. They are different because of Earth's rotations and revolutions.

Here's how it works:

Earth rotates one time each day. But Earth's axis is not straight up and down. It tilts a little. So, Earth tilts a little, too.

Earth orbits or circles the sun one time each year. That makes one revolution.

Since Earth is tilted, the sun's most direct rays strike Earth at different places depending on Earth's rotation and revolution. Some places experience daylight while other places experience nighttime. This is a result of Earth's rotations and revolutions.

Fluency Goal: Read 115 words in one minute. The highlighted word is the 115th word in the passage. See pages 12 and 13 for information on fluency.

Meta para la fluidez: Leer 115 palabras en un minuto. La palabra destacada es la palabra número 115 en la historia. ***Ver las páginas 12 y 13 para más información sobre la fluidez de la lectura.***

1. What are the four seasons?

____

____

2. How many times does Earth rotate in one day?

____

____

Comparing Numbers

Use the symbols > (greater than) and < (less than) to compare each set of numbers. Complete each sentence.

Usa los símbolos > (mayor que) y < (menor que) para comparar cada conjunto de números. Completa cada oración.

Example 9,879 (>) 9,047 9,879 is greater than 9,047.	**1.** 8,068 ◯ 8,714 8,068 is ________ than 8,714.	**2.** 9,748 ◯ 9,401 9,748 is ________ than 9,401.
3. 6,712 ◯ 6,233 6,712 is ________ than 6,233.	**4.** 5,324 ◯ 5,491 5,324 is ________ than 5,491.	**5.** 8,551 ◯ 8,753 8,551 is ________ than 8,753.
6. 2,585 ◯ 2,306 2,585 is ________ than 2,306.	**7.** 1,132 ◯ 1,906 1,132 is ________ than 1,906.	**8.** 9,149 ◯ 9,925 9,149 is ________ than 9,925.
9. 7,385 ◯ 7,636 7,385 is ________ than 7,636.	**10.** 8,102 ◯ 8,530 8,102 is ________ than 8,530.	**11.** 5,758 ◯ 5,734 5,758 is ________ than 5,734.
12. 1,866 ◯ 1,432 1,866 is ________ than 1,432.	**13.** 5,209 ◯ 5,953 5,209 is ________ than 5,953.	**14.** 6,224 ◯ 6,249 6,224 is ________ than 6,249.
15. 6,508 ◯ 6,714 6,508 is ________ than 6,714.	**16.** 1,737 ◯ 1,192 1,737 is ________ than 1,192.	**17.** 1,894 ◯ 2,712 1,894 is ________ than 2,712.

What's the Tone?

The tone of a story is the feeling it has and the feeling it makes the reader have. A tone can be happy, sad, excited, fearful, or many others.

El tono de la historia es el sentimiento que tiene y el sentimiento que hace sentir al lector. El tono puede ser feliz, triste, emocionante, aterrador, u otros más.

Word Bank

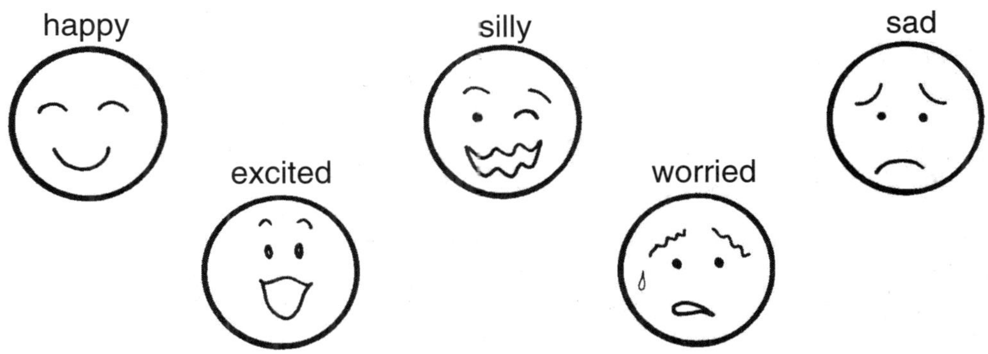

Read each paragraph below. Then write the tone of each paragraph. Choose from the words in the word bank above.

Lee los siguientes párrafos. Después escribe el tono de cada párrafo. Elige las palabras del banco de palabras anterior.

1. Wow! Today is my birthday. I know it will be a great day. We are having a chocolate cake and are playing lots of games. I can hardly wait until my friends arrive.

   Tone:______________________________

2. I can't believe my best friend is moving away. I want to cry. Even the sky looks gray and rainy today. Nothing will ever be the same without my friend.

   Tone:______________________________

3. Can a pig learn tricks? My pet pig, Sally, can roll over and shake hands. Or should I say shake snouts? She is a funny pig who really likes to "hog the show."

   Tone:______________________________

4. I can't believe our arithmetic test is today. I forgot to study, and I don't understand multiplication. I just know I will fail this test. This could ruin my math grade. Oh, why didn't I study last night?

   Tone:______________________________

5. It is a beautiful day today! The sun is shining, the birds are singing, and the air smells sweet and fresh. It feels good to be alive!

   Tone:______________________________

What Is Missing?

The subject of a sentence is the part that tells what the sentence is about. The predicate tells what the subject is doing.

Here are some sentences that are missing subjects or predicates. Choose a subject or predicate from the box to complete each sentence. Then, on the line before each number, write a **P** if you added a predicate or an **S** if you added a subject to the sentence. The first one is done for you.

El sujeto de una oración nos deja saber de qué se trata la oración. El predicado de una oración nos deja saber lo que el sujeto está haciendo.

A estas oraciones les falta el sujeto o el predicado. Elige un sujeto o predicado del cuadro para completar cada oración. Después, en el renglón delante de cada número, escribe una P si agregaste un predicado o una S si agregaste un sujeto. La primera ya está hecha.

The following subjects and predicates may be used more than once.

Los sigientes sujetos y predicados pueden ser usados más de una vez.

My teacher	The suitcase	Dinner
The mail carrier	is very gross	My bed
My kitten	is drooling	drove over the hills
has a cute little hat	An ugly grasshopper	ran on the playground
A ladybug	The tree	snores
Uncle Gerald	has an attitude	fell on my toe
My sister	is crying	is growling
A cute little baby	climbs on the furniture	is singing in an opera
	is lost in space	

_S_ 1. ______My kitten______ sat on the birthday cake.

____ 2. ________________ ate worms for breakfast.

____ 3. Laurie ________________ .

____ 4. ________________ slipped on a banana peel.

____ 5. Mrs. Crabapple ________________ .

____ 6. ________________ is a big, hairy beast.

____ 7. A giant elephant ________________ .

____ 8. My little brother ________________ .

____ 9. The grizzly bear ________________ .

____ 10. ________________ is very heavy.

Working with Money

Solve each word problem.

Resuelve los problemas escritos.

1. Kay bought 1 binder for $1.49. Kay also bought 4 erasers. The erasers sold for 2 for $0.39. How much money did Kay spend?

   $$\begin{array}{r} \$1.49 \\ \$0.39 \\ +\ \$0.39 \\ \hline \$\ 2.27 \end{array}$$

   Kay spent __$ 2.27__ .

2. Ray bought 1 calculator for $1.99, a notebook for $0.35, and 3 pencils. The pencils cost $0.10 each. How much money did Ray spend?

   Ray spent ________ .

3. Jay had $1.50. He bought a pencil sharpener for $0.22 and 2 sheets of special paper. Each sheet of paper costs $0.13. How much money did Jay have left?

   Jay had ________ left.

4. Fay had $2.00. She spent $0.15 on a notebook cover and $0.28 for a box of crayons. How much money did Fay have left?

   Fay had ________ left.

5. May bought 6 bookmarks. The bookmarks cost $0.25 for 3. May also bought a folder for $0.11. How much money did May spend?

   May spent ________ .

6. Clay bought a ruler for $0.33 and a pen for $0.10. Clay paid for the items with a one dollar bill. How much change was Clay given?

   Clay was given ________ in change.

7. Gray had $0.71. He spent $0.11 buying a notepad and $0.19 buying a small stapler. How much money did Gray have left?

   Gray had ________ left.

8. Bay bought a pencil box for $0.84, a jumbo pencil for $0.25, and a set of markers for $0.39. How much money did Bay spend?

   Bay spent ________ .

Drawing Conclusions

Read the sentences below and then answer the questions.

Lee las siguientes oraciones y luego responde las preguntas.

	Answer
1. I live on a farm. I have feathers and wings. I wake up the farm in the morning. What am I?	
2. You watch me in a large building. You see me on a screen. People eat popcorn and drink soda while I am playing. What am I?	
3. Some people use me to write, other people use me to play games, and many people use me to find information and to send messages to each other. I can be found in many homes and most businesses. What am I?	
4. I grow from the ground. I smell sweet. My stem has thorns, but I am beautiful. What am I?	
5. I make beautiful sounds. I have a long neck and strings. Some people use a pick to play me. They strum my strings, and the sound vibrates. What am I?	

Finding Perimeters of Rectangles

The perimeter is the distance around the edge of a shape. Solve each perimeter problem. Circle the correct letter.

El perímetro es la distancia alrededor del borde de una forma. Resuelve los problemas de perímetro. Encierra en un círculo la letra correcta.

1. Find the perimeter of the rectangle.

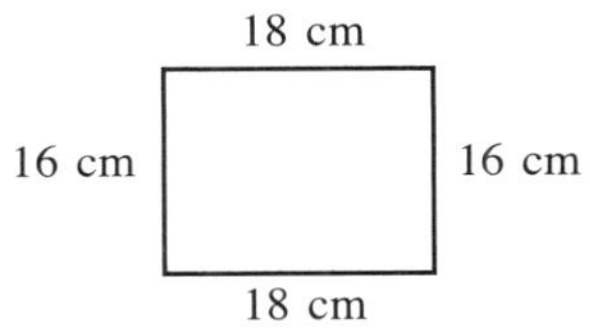

(A) 34 cm (B) 288 cm
(C) 17 cm (D) 68 cm

2. Find the perimeter of the rectangle.

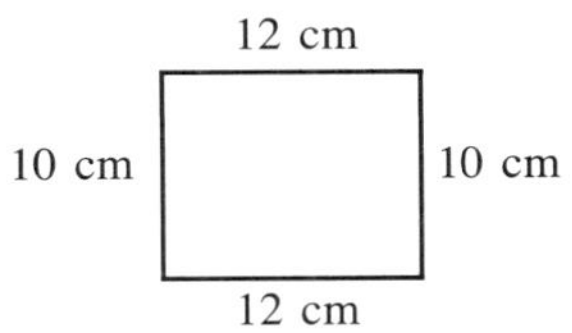

(A) 44 cm (B) 11 cm
(C) 22 cm (D) 120 cm

3. Find the perimeter of the rectangle.

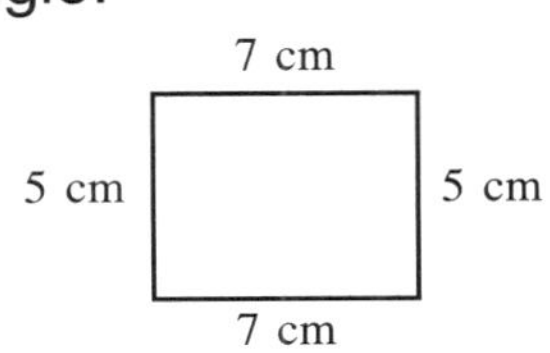

(A) 12 cm (B) 24 cm
(C) 35 cm (D) 6 cm

4. Find the perimeter of the rectangle.

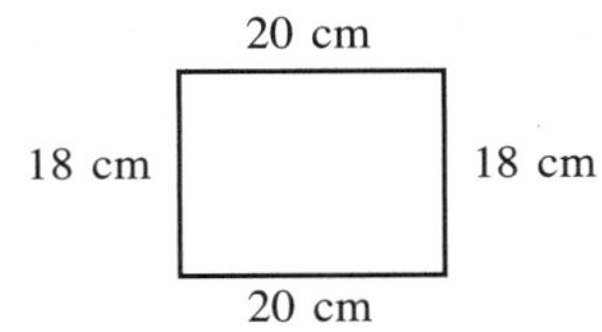

(A) 360 cm (B) 38 cm
(C) 76 cm (D) 19 cm

5. Find the perimeter of the rectangle.

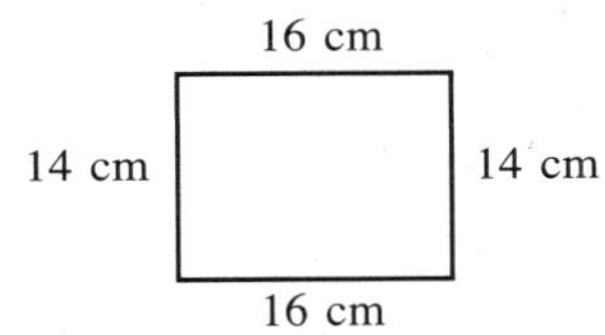

(A) 60 cm (B) 224 cm
(C) 30 cm (D) 15 cm

6. Find the perimeter of the rectangle.

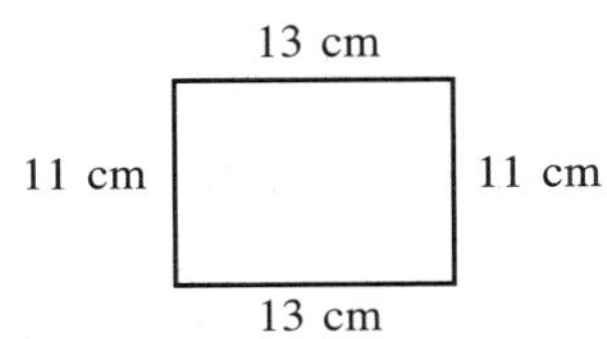

(A) 24 cm (B) 12 cm
(C) 48 cm (D) 143 cm

Three Scoops Please!

You are creating three new ice cream flavors, and must assign titles to each of these new flavors. Write a description for each new flavor using adjectives, sensory imagery, and figurative language. Illustrate your triple scoop ice cream cone to accurately depict your three new flavors.

Estás inventando tres nuevos sabores de helado, y debes darle nombre a cada uno de estos nuevos sabores. Escribe una descripción de cada sabor nuevo usando adjetivos, imágenes sensoriales y lenguaje figurativo. Ilustra tu helado de tres bolas para describir con precisión tus tres sabores nuevos.

Flavor #1: ______________________

Description: ____________________

____

____

____

____

Flavor #2: ______________________

Description: ____________________

____

____

____

____

Flavor #3: ______________________

Description: ____________________

____

____

____

____

Which Is Larger?

Shade to show the correct fraction. Then circle the larger fraction.

Sombrea para mostrar la fracción correcta. Luego encierra en un círculo la fracción más grande.

Example

$\frac{9}{12}$

$\frac{1}{2}$

1.

$\frac{3}{9}$

$\frac{4}{10}$

2.

$\frac{8}{10}$

$\frac{4}{6}$

3.

$\frac{1}{4}$

$\frac{2}{3}$

4.

$\frac{8}{9}$

$\frac{7}{8}$

5.

$\frac{2}{7}$

$\frac{5}{9}$

6.

$\frac{4}{7}$

$\frac{3}{10}$

7.

$\frac{3}{7}$

$\frac{1}{6}$

8.

$\frac{3}{4}$

$\frac{1}{5}$

9.

$\frac{3}{8}$

$\frac{1}{9}$

Challenge Project for Week 1

Innovations can be created from poems, stories, or books by substituting nouns, verbs, and adjectives to fit a new context. For example, if the original story is set in the jungle, an innovation could be written about the oceans. Different animal names and descriptive words would be substituted to reflect the new setting. Follow the steps below to write your own innovation.

Las innovaciones se pueden crear a partir de poemas, historias o libros sustituyendo sustantivos, verbos y adjetivos para adaptarlos a un nuevo contexto. Por ejemplo, si la historia original sucede en la selva, se puede escribir una innovación sobre los océanos. Se sustituirán nombres de animales y palabras descriptivas para reflejar el nuevo lugar. Sigue estos pasos para escribir tu propia innovación.

Directions

1. Decide on a story to innovate.

   Decide sobre una historia para innovar.

2. Determine the new setting of the story.

   Determina el nuevo escenario de la historia.

3. Brainstorm lists of words for the new setting—animals, plants, sounds, descriptive words and phrases, etc. Use these words to replace specified words in the chosen text.

   Piensa en listas de palabras para el nuevo ajuste -- animales, plantas, sonidos, palabras y frases descriptivas, etc. Usa estas palabras para substituir palabras especificadas en el texto elegido.

4. Write one to four sentences on each sheet of paper. Illustrate each page. Compile the pages to make a book.

   Escribe de una a cuatro oraciones en cada hoja del papel. Ilustra cada página. Compila las páginas para hacer un libro.

Example based on *The Great Kapok Tree* by Lynn Cherry.

Ejemplo basado en el libro The Great Kapok Tree por Lynn Cherry.

Lights!

Camera!

Action!!!

____

(Name)

Has successfully completed

Week 1

of

Kids Learn.

Congratulations!

____

(Date)

Vacation Time!

When places are written with a name, they need capital letters because they are proper nouns.

Cuando escribas nombres de lugares, necesitan letras mayúsculas porque son sustantivos propios.

Capitalize the names of special places.
Escribe con mayúscula los nombres de sitios especiales.

Here is a list of places that need capital letters. Correct the letters that need to be capitalized. Then choose three of the places you would like to visit.

Esta es una lista de lugares que necesitan letras mayúsculas. Corrige las letras que deben ir en mayúscula. Después elige tres lugares que te gustaría visitar.

1. pacific Ocean
2. Grand canyon
3. Mt. rushmore
4. amazon River
5. san diego Zoo
6. hyde park
7. sahara desert
8. lake Louise
9. disneyland
10. North pole
11. rocky Mountains
12. niagara falls

I would like to visit the following places.

Me gustaría visitar los siguientes lugares.

1. ______________________________
2. ______________________________
3. ______________________________

Name your favorite place to visit. Write something about this place.

Nombra tu lugar favorito para visitar. Escribe algo acerca de este lugar.

____

____

____

____

____

____

What Is Closer?

When rounding to the nearest ten, check the number in the ones place.

Cuando estés redondeando a la decena, revisa el número de las unidades.

- If the number is 5 or greater, round up. Example: 47 → 50
- If the number is 4 or less, round down. Example: 43 → 40

Round each number to the nearest ten.

Redondea cada número a la decena más cercana.

1. 85 90	**4.** 6 ____	**7.** 82 ____	**10.** 24 ____
2. 19 ____	**5.** 14 ____	**8.** 7 ____	**11.** 17 ____
3. 73 ____	**6.** 69 ____	**9.** 13 ____	**12.** 5 ____

When rounding to the nearest hundred, check the number in the tens place.

Cuando estés redondeando a la centena, revisa el número en el lugar de las decenas.

- If the number is 5 or greater, round up. Example: 158 → 200
- If the number is 4 or less, round down. Example: 132 → 100

Round each number to the nearest hundred.

Redondea cada número a la centena más cercana.

13. 176 200	**16.** 295 ______	**19.** 417 ______	**22.** 323 ______
14. 451 ______	**17.** 945 ______	**20.** 897 ______	**23.** 183 ______
15. 108 ______	**18.** 557 ______	**21.** 827 ______	**24.** 442 ______

When rounding to the nearest thousand, check the number in the hundreds place.

Cuando estés redondeando al millar, revisa el número en el lugar de las centenas.

- If the number is 5 or greater, round up. Example: 1,903 → 2,000
- If the number is 4 or less, round down. Example: 1,499 → 1,000

Round each number to the nearest thousand.

Redondea cada número al millar más cercano.

25. 5,929 6,000	**28.** 1,149 ________	**31.** 7,028 ________	**34.** 4,359 ________
26. 7,463 ________	**29.** 1,771 ________	**32.** 8,932 ________	**35.** 2,449 ________
27. 1,043 ________	**30.** 6,416 ________	**33.** 8,422 ________	**36.** 2,822 ________

Recognizing Details

Read the reading passage. Then answer the questions below.

Lee el cuento y responde a las preguntas.

Redwoods

Redwood trees are one of the longest-living plants on Earth. Many have already lived more than 2,000 years. Almost nothing can kill them. They do not die from disease. Bugs and fungi do not kill them. During a forest fire, the tree's bark may burn, but it will still survive. The same happens when lightning strikes. Over many years, the tree will slowly regrow the bark and heal the scars. Those trees blown down by strong winds send up shoots from their roots. After a redwood tree is cut down, its stump will send up shoots.

What is the main idea? Fill in the bubble that tells the main idea.

Llena la burbuja que indica la idea principal.

ⓐ Redwood trees live longer than any other plant or animal on Earth.

ⓑ Redwood trees do not die easily.

ⓒ After a redwood tree is cut down, its stump will send up shoots.

Name several details that support the main idea.

Da varios detalles que apoyan la idea principal.

1. ________________________________
2. ________________________________
3. ________________________________
4. ________________________________
5. ________________________________
6. ________________________________
7. ________________________________
8. ________________________________

Rounding Numbers to Estimate Answers

Estimate each word problem by rounding each number to the nearest ten and then adding or subtracting. Show your work in the space provided.

Resuelve los problemas escritos redondeando cada número a la decena más cercana y sumando o restando después. Muestra tu trabajo en el espacio.

1. Jason invited 39 girls and 22 boys to his party. How many children did Jason invite in all? The number 39 is rounded to 40. The number 22 is rounded to 20. (40 + 20 = 60) About __60__ children in all were invited to the party.	40 + 20 60
2. Mariah bought 152 balloons, 127 party hats, and 213 candles for the party. How many party items did Mariah buy in all? Mariah bought about _____ party items in all.	
3. Beau sent out 185 invitations. 87 people said "yes." The rest said "no." How many people said "no"? About _____ people said "no."	
4. Lucy set out 210 green jellybeans, 315 red jellybeans, and 57 orange jellybeans. How many jellybeans did Lucy set out in all? Lucy set out about _____ jellybeans in all.	
5. Sprinkles were put on 3 cupcakes. The children used 567 sprinkles in all. The first cupcake had 237 sprinkles. The second cupcake had 197. How many sprinkles did the third cupcake have? The third cupcake had about _____ sprinkles.	
6. Darts were played at the party. Ben scored 222 points. Jacob scored 303 points. Elena scored 368 points. How many points were scored in all? About _____ points were scored in all.	

Articles: A and An

Articles are a kind of adjective. The three most common articles are the, a, and an. A is used before words that begin with a consonant sound. An is used before words that begin with a vowel sound.

Los artículos son un tipo de adjetivo. Los tres más comunes en inglés son the, a, y an. A es usado antes de las palabras que comienzan con una consonante. An es usado antes de palabras que comienzan con una vocal.

a house

an apple

Write **a** or **an** in the blanks below.

Escribe a o an en los siguientes espacios vacíos.

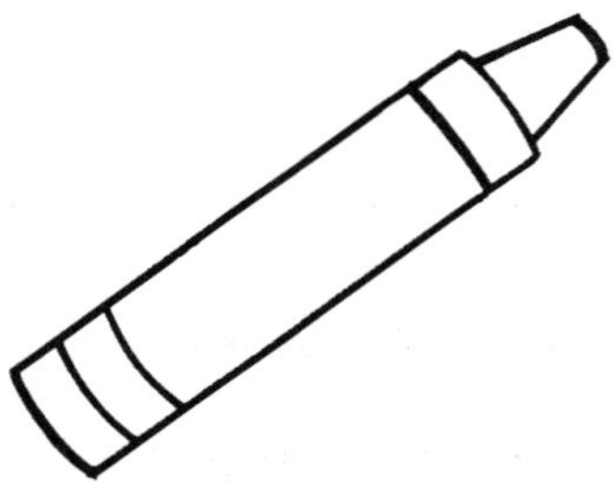

1. _______ crayon
2. _______ ape
3. _______ saucer
4. _______ egg
5. _______ monkey
6. _______ pill
7. _______ itch
8. _______ orange
9. _______ blouse
10. _______ log
11. _________ ant crawled across the leaf.
12. Have you seen _________ purple butterfly?
13. I would like to eat _________ sandwich for lunch.
14. _________ apple a day keeps the doctor away.
15. _________ goat chewed on my pant leg!

Out of This World

For this fictional narrative assignment, you will create a new planet in our solar system and write a narrative about this planet.

Para esta tarea de narración de ficción, inventa un planeta nuevo en nuestro sistema solar y escribe una narración sobre ese planeta.

Use the template below as a prewriting guide.

Illustration of planet

Name of planet ______________________________

Reason for name______________________________

Planet's shape and size ______________________

Position in the solar system __________________

Climate ____________________________________

Topography _________________________________

Atmosphere _________________________________

Life forms__________________________________

Vegetation _________________________________

Now write a paragraph about the new planet. Use your prewriting to help you.

Ahora escribe un párrafo sobre el planeta nuevo. Usa tu escritura previa para ayudarte.

Buying Things

Use the chart to help solve each word problem. Fill in the correct answer circle.

Usa esta tabla como ayuda para resolver los problemas escritos. Llena el círculo de la respuesta correcta.

stamps	big envelopes	small envelopes	bubble wrap
 37¢	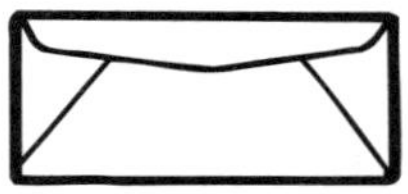 12¢	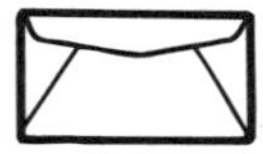 8¢	 11¢ per foot
pens	**small box**	**medium-size box**	**big box**
 2 for 15¢	 25¢	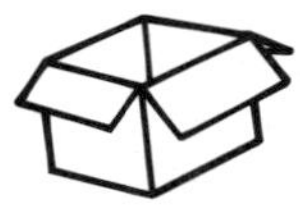 40¢	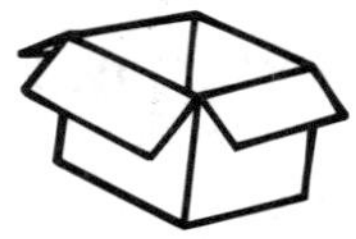 55¢

1. Jamal bought 4 pens, 3 stamps, and 5 feet of bubble wrap. How much money did Jamal spend?

   $0.15 + 0.15 = $ .30 pens; $ .37 + .37 + .37 = $ 1.11 stamps; $ .11 + .11 + .11 + .11 + .11 = $ .55 bubble wrap; $ .30 + $ 1.11 + $ .55 = $ 1.96 total

   ○ $0.96 ● $1.96 ○ $2.96

2. Wendy bought 2 medium-size boxes, 5 small envelopes and 1 big envelope. How much money did Wendy spend?

   ○ $1.32 ○ $1.23 ○ $13.20

3. Kevin bought 8 feet of bubble wrap, 6 pens, 1 stamp, and 1 big box. How much money did Kevin spend?

   ○ $2.25 ○ $2.15 ○ $2.05

4. Adriana bought 2 small boxes, 4 big envelopes, and 4 stamps. How much money did Adriana spend?

   ○ $2.34 ○ $2.46 ○ $3.24

Character Web

You can see this is a special kind of web. It is a character web.

Read a book. Draw a picture of the main character in the center circle. In each of the spaces, answer the question about the character.

Puedes ver que ésta es una tela de araña especial. Es una tela de araña de personaje.

Lee un libro. Haz un dibujo del personaje principal en el círculo del centro. En cada uno de los espacios, contesta la pregunta sobre el personaje.

Categorizing

In the word box below are 42 words, each of which belongs in one of the six categories—wood, metals, water, space, colors, or furniture. Place each of the words under the correct category. For example, **bay** would belong in the **water** category. Seven words belong under each category.

En el siguiente cuadro hay 42 palabras. Cada una corresponde a una de seis categorías: wood (madera), metals (metales), water (agua), space (espacio), colors (colores) o furniture (muebles). Coloca cada palabra debajo de la categoría correcta. Por ejemplo, bay corresponde a la categoría water. En cada categoría debe haber siete palabras.

bay	lumber	dresser	chest	steel	iron	chartreuse
Mars	tin	tan	pond	blue	forest	aluminum
rocket	mirror	scarlet	orbit	green	nail	weightless
creek	oak	bronze	board	river	rocker	countdown
sea	lake	red	cabinet	beige	walnut	pencil
lamp	ocean	moon	couch	copper	astronaut	maple

wood	**metals**	**water**
______	______	______
______	______	______
______	______	______
______	______	______
______	______	______
______	______	______
______	______	______

space	**colors**	**furniture**
______	______	______
______	______	______
______	______	______
______	______	______
______	______	______
______	______	______
______	______	______

Comparing Numbers on a Chart

The data in the box below is taken from dietary sheets provided by McDonald's™ restaurants. Read through the data box and use the information provided to figure out which side of each inequality has the greater number of calories. Place a < or > sign in the space provided to complete each problem.

La información del siguiente cuadro viene de la hoja nutricional de los restaurantes McDonald's™. Lee los datos y usa la información para descubrir qué lado de cada desigualdad tiene la mayor cantidad de calorías. Coloca un signo < ó > en el espacio para completar cada problema.

These figures reflect the number of calories in each item.

hamburger—270

cheeseburger—320

fish sandwich—360

small french fries—210

garden salad—80

hot fudge sundae—290

apple pie—260

1% milk—100

small soda—150

chocolate shake—340

1. 2 hamburgers (<) 2 hot fudge sundaes
2. 1 fish sandwich ◯ 4 garden salads
3. 5 small sodas ◯ 3 fish sandwiches
4. 3 chocolate shakes ◯ 12 1% milks
5. 2 apple pies ◯ 7 garden salads
6. 3 cheeseburgers ◯ 5 small french fries
7. 2 garden salads + 3 cheeseburgers ◯ 4 hamburgers
8. 4 fish sandwiches ◯ 6 small french fries + 1 garden salad
9. 2 small sodas + 1 chocolate shake ◯ 2 apple pies + 3 1% milks
10. 2 hot fudge sundaes ◯ 2 small french fries + 3 garden salads
11. 6 1% milks + 2 cheeseburgers ◯ 4 small french fries + 1 shake
12. 2 apple pies + 2 fish sandwiches ◯ 3 cheeseburgers + 3 small french fries

Challenge Project for Week 2

Number 10 index cards or pieces of paper from 0–9. Shuffle the number cards and place them in a stack facedown. Turn over the top five cards and lay them out in the order they were turned over. Record the numbers. Write whether the number made is odd or even. (Remember, odd numbers end in 1, 3, 5, 7, or 9 and even numbers end in 0, 2, 4, 6, or 8.) Write the numbers that come before and after the number made. The first one has been done for you.

Numera 10 trozos de papel o tarjetas del 0 al 9. Mézclalas y colócalas en un montón cara abajo. Saca cinco tarjetas de arriba y colócalas en el orden en que les diste vuelta. Registra los números. Escribe si el número que salió es par o impar. (Recuerda: los números impares terminan en 1, 3, 5, 7 o 9 y los números pares terminan en 0, 2, 4, 6 o 8.) Escribe los números que vienen antes y después del número que salió. El primero ya está hecho.

	number made with the cards	odd or even	number that comes before	number that comes after
1.	3 6 , 9 0 8	even	36,907	36,909
2.	,			
3.	,			
4.	,			
5.	,			
6.	,			
7.	,			
8.	,			

Let's Celebrate!

____

(Name)

has completed

Week 2

of Kids Learn!

____

(Date)

Punctuation Challenge

Read the letter. There are 21 punctuation errors. Circle the punctuation that is wrong and correct it. Add any missing punctuation.

Lee la carta. Hay 21 errores de puntuación. Encierra en un círculo cada error y corrígelo. Agrega la puntuación que falte.

Dear Pen Pal,

I love to go to the circus! On May 6 1999, the circus came to my hometown of Jackson Wyoming. A parade marched through our streets and soon the big top could be seen. Ken my best friend, and I went to watch the performers prepare for opening night. We saw clowns, acrobats, and even the ringmaster. What a sight? Have you ever seen anything like it. You should go if you ever get the chance.

I also really enjoy playing baseball. My favorite team is the New York Yankees but I also like the St. Louis Cardinals. When I grow up, I want to be a baseball pitcher, first baseman, or shortstop. Do you like baseball? What do you want to do when you grow up. I wish you could see my cool baseball card collection, but Kens collection is even better.

Oh, I almost forgot to tell you about my family! There are four people in my family. They are my mom my dad my brother and me. Scruffy my cat is also a family member. In August 2000 my grandpa will probably move in with us. I cant wait for that! Didn't you say your grandma lives with you. Ill bet you really like that.

Well thats all for now. Please, write back to me soon. See you!

Your pal,

Brent

Fractions and Money

Complete the chart.

Completa la tabla.

Coin	Number Needed to Make $1.00	Fraction of $1.00
1. half dollar	2	1/2 of a $1.00
2. quarters		
3. dimes		
4. nickels		
5. pennies		

Write each amount using a dollar sign and a decimal point.

Escribe cada cantidad usando el signo de dólares y un punto decimal.

6. Four dollars eighty-three cents ____________
7. Thirty-nine dollars seventy-six cents ____________
8. Two hundred eighty-one dollars ten cents ____________

Read each word problem. Write the money in two ways—as a fraction of a dollar and with a dollar sign and decimal point.

Lee cada problema escrito. Escribe el dinero de dos maneras: como fracción de un dólar y con un signo de dólar y punto decimal.

9. Gloria has 5 dimes, 1 nickel, and 6 pennies.

   61 /100 or $ ___. 6 1

10. Sean has 2 quarters, 2 nickels, and 5 pennies.

    _____/100 or $ ___. ___ ___

11. Linda has 8 dimes and 7 nickels.

    _____/100 or $ ___. ___ ___

12. Bart has 1 half dollar, 1 quarter, and 10 pennies.

    _____/100 or $ ___. ___ ___

Thesaurus Practice

Here is an entry from a thesaurus. Use it to answer the questions.

Aquí está una entrada de un tesauro. Úsala para contestar las siguientes preguntas.

close: *adj.* 1. beside, near, by
2. *Ant.* far (away) from

close: *v.* 1. lock, close up, shut
2. *Ant.* open, unlock

1. **You can tell from this thesaurus entry that things that are close**
   A. have little space between them.
   B. are very far apart from each other.
   C. look exactly the same.
   D. are the opposite of each other.

Read this sentence.

Lee esta oración.

It is very important to close the door when you leave the classroom.

2. **Which *synonym* (same) could be used to replace the word close in the sentence?**
   A. unlock
   B. shut
   C. open
   D. near

Read this sentence.

Lee esta oración.

I like to sit close to my friends during lunch.

3. **Which *antonym* (opposite) could be used to replace the words close to in the sentence?**
   A. next to
   B. by
   C. beside
   D. far from

Identifying the Speaker

Read the story and answer the questions below.

Lee la historia y responde las siguientes preguntas.

Tracy had a big surprise when he took the trash out one night. He saw a small, furry animal hanging upside down in the trash can. Its body was covered in fuzzy gray fur and its tail had black stripes. "Get out of there!" yelled Tracy.

"What is going on?" called his father from inside the house.

"Raccoons are hunting in our garbage," said the boy. The raccoons always seemed to be getting into the trash cans. He went back into the house and got a broom to chase the raccoons away. But when he came back, the furry raccoons were already gone. "I guess I'd better make sure that the lid is on tightly," he said.

Fluency Goal: Read 115 words in one minute. The highlighted word is the 115th word in the passage. See pages 12 and 13 for information on fluency.

Meta para la fluidez: Leer 115 palabras en un minuto. La palabra destacada es la palabra número 115 en la historia. ***Ver las páginas 12 y 13 para más información sobre la fluidez de la lectura.***

1. How many speakers are in the story? ______________________________

2. Who are the speakers? ______________________________

3. Who said that he should make sure that the lid was on tightly?

   ____

4. How do you know Tracy is a boy? ______________________________

   ____

Basic Geometry

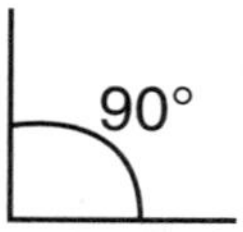 **Right Angle** A right angle makes a corner. A right angle is 90°.	 **Acute Angle** An acute angle is < 90° (is less than 90°).	 **Obtuse Angle** An obtuse angle is > 90° (is greater than 90°).

Circle the answer that best describes the angle.

Encierra en un círculo la respuesta que mejor describa el ángulo.

1.

< 90° 90° > 90°

2.

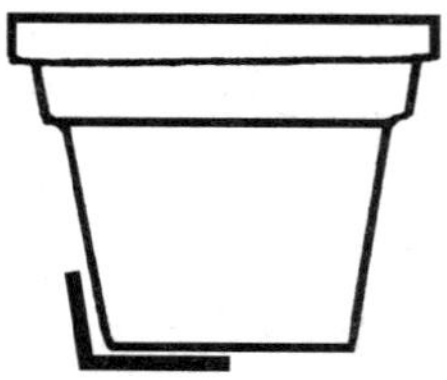

< 90° 90° > 90°

3.

< 90° 90° > 90°

Follow the directions.

Sigue las instrucciones.

4. Circle the *right* triangle.
5. Draw a line under the *obtuse* triangle.
6. Make an x on the *acute* triangle.

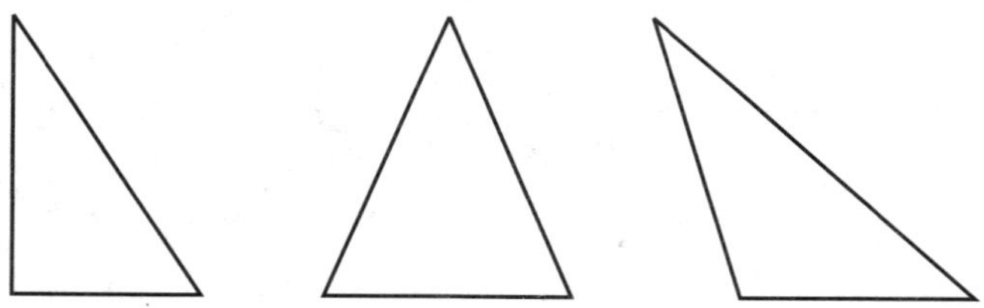

equilateral

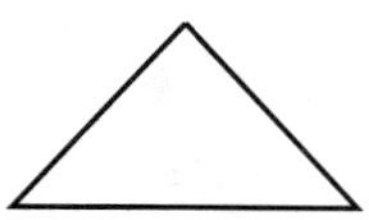

isosceles

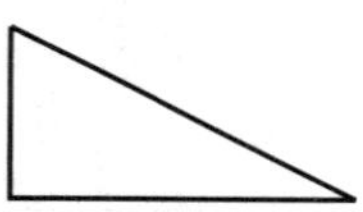

scalene

Which Triangle Am I?

7. Only two of my sides are congruent (equal in length). Which triangle am I? ______________________
8. None of my sides are congruent (equal in length). Which shape am I? ______________________
9. All of my sides are congruent (equal in length). Which shape am I? ______________________

Let Me Tell You

A topic sentence tells what a paragraph is all about. Write a topic sentence for each paragraph below.

Una oración temática te dice de lo que se tratará un párrafo. Escribe una oración temática para cada párrafo a continuación.

____

____

____

There are lions and tigers in outdoor pens. Wild birds are flying in large, tree-filled cages. Also, a visitor at the zoo can see snakes and reptiles of many different sizes. My favorite thing to see at the zoo is the monkey that swings on a trapeze in a cage by the popcorn stand.

____

____

____

First, you must listen carefully in class. Next, you must study for your tests and quizzes. Finally, you must do all the homework the teacher assigns. If you follow these steps, good grades will be yours!

____

____

____

It starts slowly and then destroys everything in its way. It can ruin homes and land. It can kill people and animals. So before you strike a match, remember how dangerous fire can be.

Check your paragraphs. Do all of your topic sentences make sense in the paragraph? Do all the sentences relate to each topic sentence?

Revisa tus párrafos. ¿Todas tus oraciones temáticas tienen sentido en el párrafo? ¿Todas las oraciones se relacionan con cada oración temática?

Brush Up on Root Words

On each brush is a word with a prefix or a suffix. Find the root word in each and write it on the tooth. (Example: farmer, farm)

Cada cepillo tiene una palabra con un prefijo o un sufijo. Encuentra la palabra raíz de cada una y escríbela en el diente. (Por ejemplo: "farmer, farm")

1. 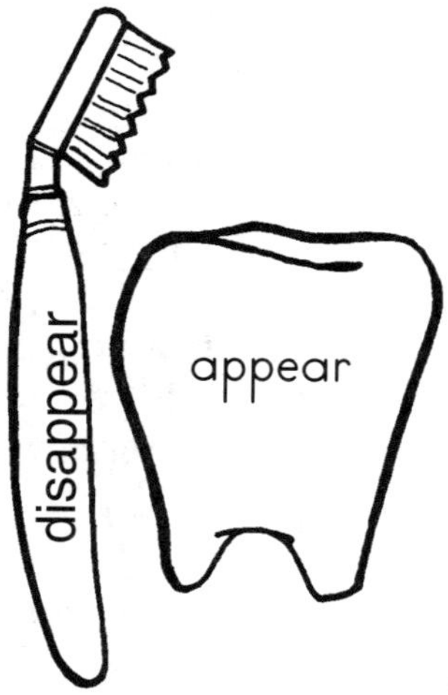

2. 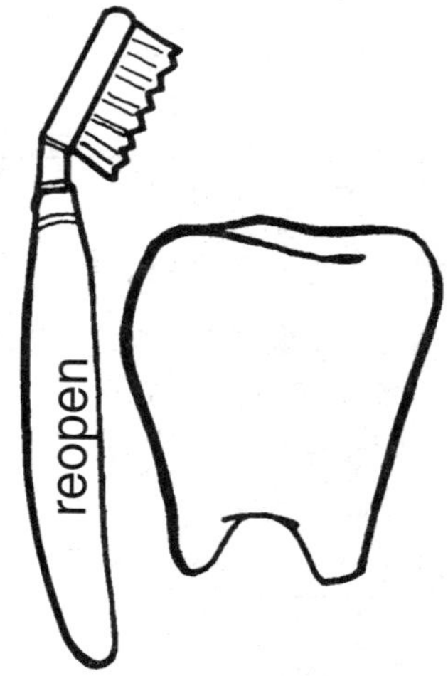

3. 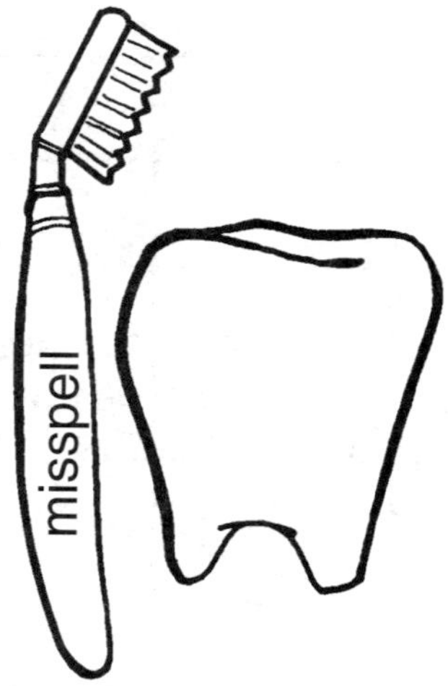

4. 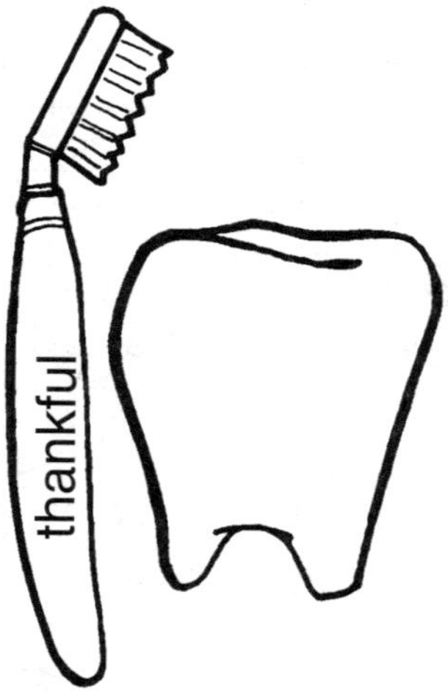

5. 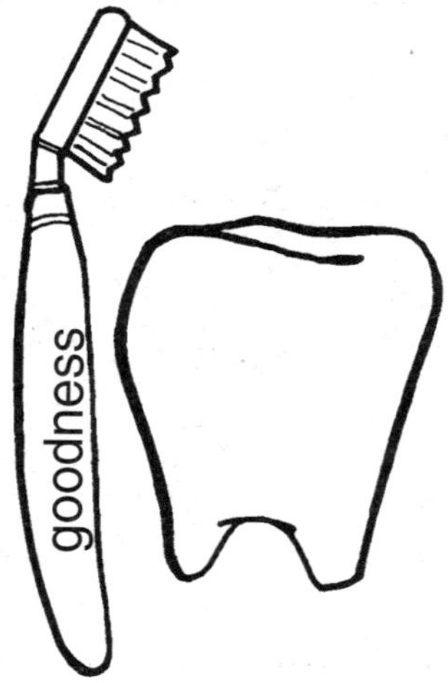

6. 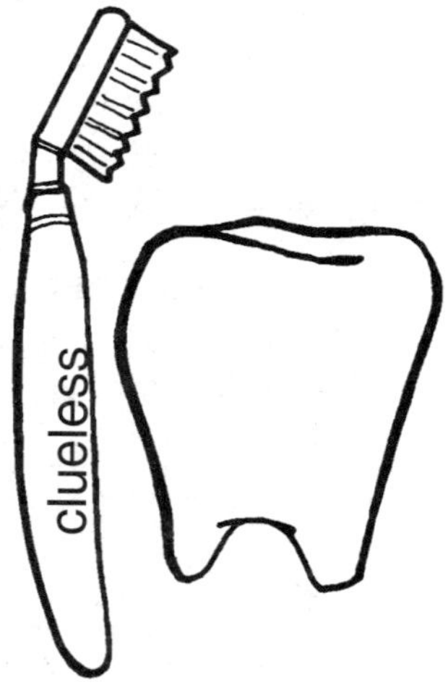

7. 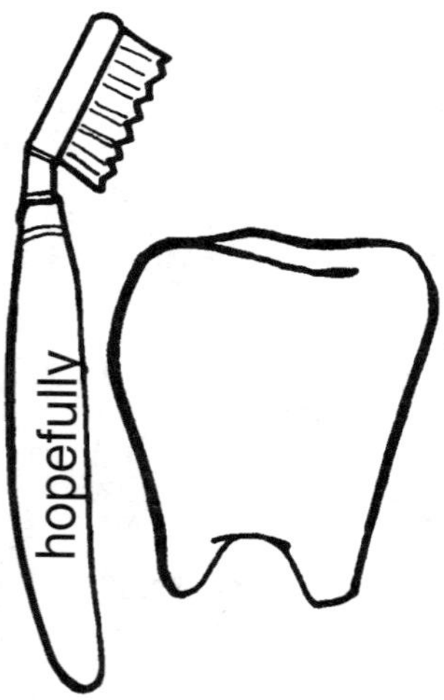

8. 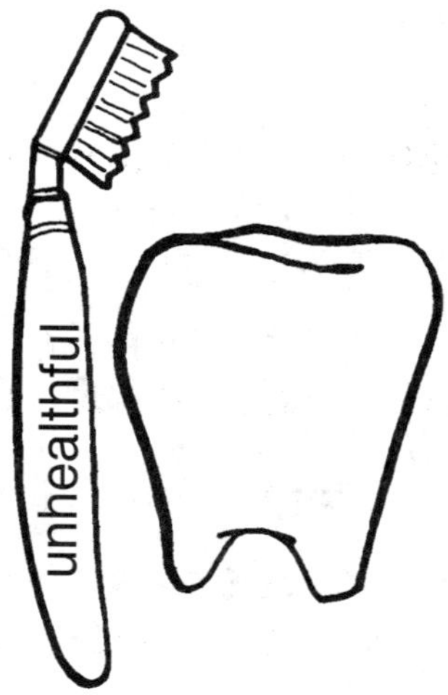

9. 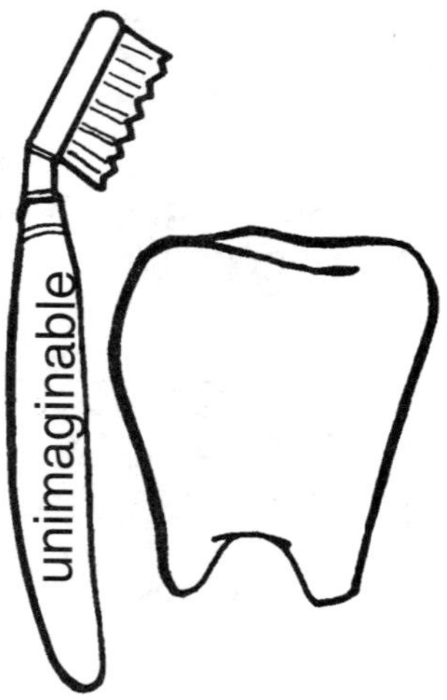

Multiplication

Solve each multiplication problem. Use each answer's letter to discover a secret question and its answer.

Resuelve cada problema de multiplicación. Usa la letra de cada respuesta para descubrir una pregunta secreta y su respuesta.

1. 14 x 2 = 28 = W	2. 331 x 2 = I	3. 4,244 x 2 = T	4. 321 x 3 = N	5. 212 x 4 = L
6. 3,412 x 2 = M	7. 313 x 3 = A	8. 441 x 2 = H	9. 3,142 x 2 = P	10. 2,211 x 4 = ?
11. 324 x 2 = U	12. 2,332 x 3 = C	13. 1,322 x 3 = !	14. 1,241 x 2 = Y	15. 4,123 x 2 = O

W___ ___ ___   ___ ___ ___
28 882 8,246   6,996 939 963

___ ___ ___ ___ ___ ___ ___ ___ ___
6,824 648 848 8,488 662 6,284 848 2,482 8,844

___   ___ ___ ___ ___
662   6,996 939 963 3,966

What Is a Sentence?

A sentence begins with a capital letter and ends with a period (.), a question mark (?), or an exclamation point (!).

Una oración comienza con una letra mayúscula y termina con un punto (.), un signo de pregunta (?), o un signo de exclamación (!).

A sentence can be a group of words that tells us something.

Una oración puede ser un grupo de palabras que nos dice algo.

Examples: Jacob went to the beach.

I won first prize!

A sentence can also be a group of words that asks us a question.

Una oración también puede ser un grupo de palabras que nos hace una pregunta.

Example: When did Nancy leave?

A sentence is always a complete thought.

Una oración siempre es una idea completa.

Circle the complete sentences below. Remember that each sentence must start with a capital letter; end with a period, question mark, or exclamation point; and be a complete thought.

Encierra en un círculo las siguientes oraciones completas. Recuerda que cada oración debe de comenzar con una mayúscula, terminar con un punto, un signo de pregunta, o uno de exclamación, y ser una idea completa.

1. over the rainbow!
2. Becky writes a letter.
3. What does Jaime want?
4. strawberries and bananas
5. Watch out for the ball!
6. when school over?
7. I am in the pool.
8. When Derek
9. Do you like dogs?
10. I can see you!
11. If I stop
12. a house on the hill
13. why don't you
14. I painted my brother green.
15. It made my mom laugh.

Equivalent Fractions

Shade in the correct amount on each circle to show the equivalent fractions.

Llena la cantidad correcta en cada círculo para mostrar las fracciones equivalentes.

1.

$\frac{1}{2} = \frac{3}{6}$

2.

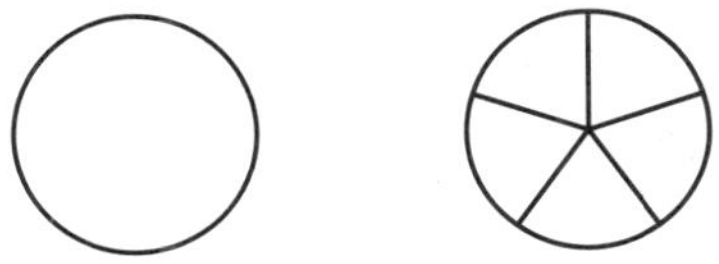

$\frac{1}{1} = \frac{5}{5}$

3.

$\frac{2}{3} = \frac{6}{9}$

4.

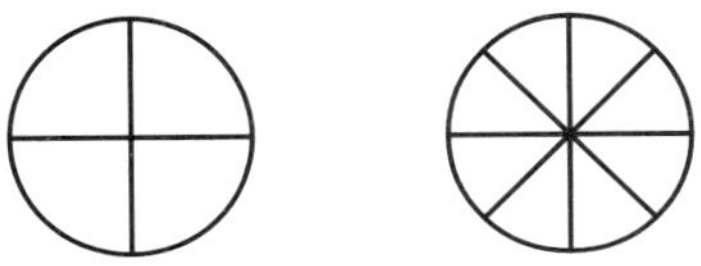

$\frac{2}{4} = \frac{4}{8}$

5.

$\frac{1}{3} = \frac{2}{6}$

6.

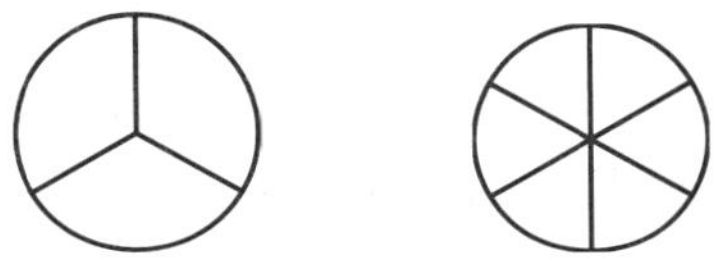

$\frac{2}{3} = \frac{4}{6}$

Shade in the correct amount on each circle. Then use the > (greater than), < (less than), or = (equal to) symbols to compare each set of fractions.

Llena la cantidad correcta en cada círculo. Después usa los signos de > (mayor que), < (menor que), o = (igual) para comparar cada conjunto de fracciones.

7.

$\frac{2}{5}$ (<) $\frac{8}{9}$

8.

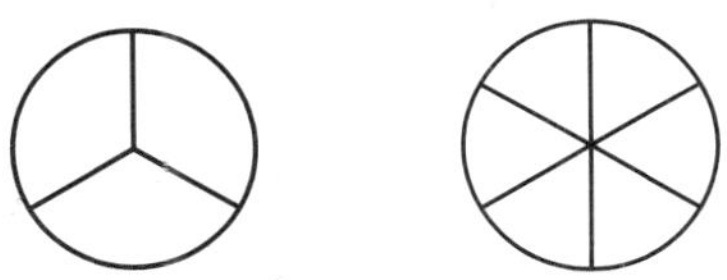

$\frac{1}{3}$ ◯ $\frac{1}{6}$

9.

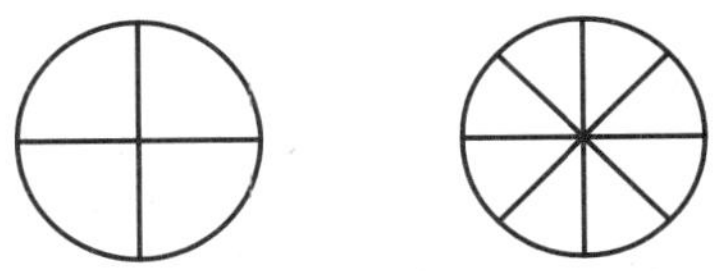

$\frac{1}{4}$ ◯ $\frac{2}{8}$

10.

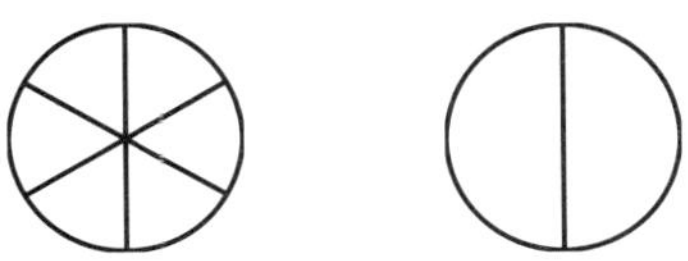

$\frac{3}{6}$ ◯ $\frac{1}{2}$

11.

$\frac{1}{1}$ ◯ $\frac{6}{7}$

12.

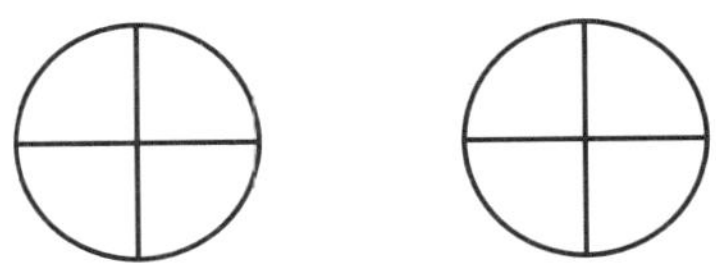

$\frac{2}{4}$ ◯ $\frac{3}{4}$

Challenge Project for Week 3

Follow the steps below to find out about how coupons can help save money.

Sigue los pasos a continuación para averiguar cómo se puede ahorrar dinero con los cupones.

- Find several coupons (3–5). Coupons are easily accessible in the newspaper or local grocery store.

  Encuentra algunos cupones (3–5). Los cupones se pueden encontrar fácilmente en el periódico o en un mercado local.

- Read the coupons. Compare and contrast information that is located on the coupons. Make a list of the information that is located on all of the coupons.

  Lee los cupones. Compara y contrasta la información localizada en los cupones. Haz una lista de la información localizada en todos los cupones.

- Look in newspaper advertisements or at local stores to find out the actual cost of the products.

  Mira en los anuncios del periódico o en tiendas locales para ver los precios actuales de los productos.

- Figure out the new cost of each item once you apply the discount of the coupon.

  Calcula el precio nuevo para cada artículo ya que apliques el descuento del cupón.

- Some stores double the value of the discount of a coupon. Figure out the cost of each item if the store in which you used the coupons doubled the value.

  Algunas tiendas doblan el valor del descuento de un cupón. Calcula el precio de cada artículo si la tienda en la cual usaste los cupones dobló el valor.

- Next, design your own coupon in the box at the bottom of the page. You can choose what product the coupon will discount. Be sure to include information that appears on most products.

  Luego, diseña tu propio cupón en la caja de abajo. Puedes escoger el producto que el cupón descontará. Asegúrate de incluir la información que aparece en la mayoría de los productos.

Read
All About It!

____

(Name)

has completed
Week 3
of
Kids Learn!

____

(Date)

Making Contractions

Write a contraction for each set of words.

Escribe una contracción para cada conjunto de palabras.

Example: would not = wouldn't

1. can not ____________
2. he is ____________
3. will not ____________
4. does not ____________
5. they are ____________
6. we are ____________
7. should not ____________
8. it will ____________

Write the words that make the contraction.

Escribe las palabras que forman la contracción.

Example: we'll = we will

9. she'll ____________
10. it's ____________
11. mustn't ____________
12. you're ____________
13. they'll ____________
14. haven't ____________
15. I'll ____________
16. I'm ____________

Write two sentences. Use at least one contraction in each.

Escribe dos oraciones. Usa por lo menos una contracción en cada una.

____

____

____

____

____

Which Word?

Homophones are words that sound the same but are spelled differently and have different meanings.

Los homófonos son palabras que suenan igual pero que se deletrean diferente y tienen significados diferentes.

8

Jim **ate eight** slices of pizza today!

Circle the correct homophone to use in each sentence. Then, write the word on the line.

Encierra en un círculo el homófono correcto que debe usarse en cada oración. Después, escribe la palabra en el renglón.

pail	**pale**	1. They collected sea shells in the ___pail___.
Two	**To**	2. ____________ friends went to the concert.
here	**hear**	3. Do you ____________ that noise?
wear	**where**	4. I am going to ____________ my new sweater.
so	**sew**	5. He will have to ____________ his button onto his shirt.
hi	**high**	6. The snow fell ____________ in the mountains.
wood	**would**	7. Collect some ____________ for the fire.
be	**bee**	8. A honey ____________ flew to the hive.
blew	**blue**	9. The wind ____________ across the water.
knew	**new**	10. I ____________ you would come!

Reading and Writing Whole Numbers

Answer each question by circling the letter of the best answer.

Responde a cada pregunta encerrando con un círculo la letra de la respuesta correcta.

1. What is the word name for 551?

(A) five hundred fifty-one

(B) five hundred five one

(C) five fifty-one

(D) five hundreds, fifty tens, and one one

2. What is the word name for 335?

(A) three hundreds, thirty tens, and five ones

(B) three hundred thirty-five

(C) three thirty-five

(D) three hundred three five

3. What is the word name for 676?

(A) six hundred seventy-six

(B) six hundred seven six

(C) six seventy-six

(D) six hundreds, seventy tens, and six ones

4. What is the word name for 717?

(A) seven hundreds, ten tens, and seven ones

(B) seven seventeen

(C) seven hundred seventeen

(D) seven hundred one seven

5. What is the word name for 168?

(A) one sixty-eight

(B) one hundred six eight

(C) one hundred sixty-eight

(D) one hundred, sixty tens, and eight ones

6. What is the word name for 993?

(A) nine hundred nine three

(B) nine ninety-three

(C) nine hundred ninety-three

(D) nine hundreds, ninety tens, and three ones

7. What is the word name for 244?

(A) two forty-four

(B) two hundred forty-four

(C) two hundreds, forty tens, and four ones

(D) two hundred four four

8. What is the word name for 829?

(A) eight hundred two nine

(B) eight twenty-nine

(C) eight hundreds, twenty tens, and nine ones

(D) eight hundred twenty-nine

9. What is the word name for 482?

(A) four eighty-two

(B) four hundred eighty-two

(C) four hundred eight two

(D) four hundreds, eighty tens, and two ones

10. What is the word name for 161?

(A) one hundred sixty-one

(B) one hundred six one

(C) one hundred, sixty tens, and one one

(D) one sixty-one

Opinion

A **fact** is a statement that can be proven and that everyone accepts as true. An **opinion** is one person's idea. Everyone does not have to accept that it is correct.

Read the story. Use a red pen or pencil to underline the sentences that are facts. Use a green pen or pencil to underline the sentences that are opinions.

Un hecho es una afirmación que se puede comprobar y que todos aceptan como verdadero. Una opinión es lo que piensa una persona. No todos tienen que aceptar que una opinión sea correcta.

Lee la historia. Subraya con una pluma o un lápiz rojo las oraciones que indican hechos. Subraya con una pluma o un lápiz verde las oraciones que indican opiniones.

A Visit to the Zoo

"I think panthers are beautiful!" exclaimed Haley.

"They are scary," said Ellen.

"Panthers belong to the cat family," said Courtney. "They weigh more than 100 pounds."

"A panther would be a great pet," Haley added.

"No, it wouldn't," announced Courtney. "It is against the law to keep a wild animal as a pet."

"This is the best trip we have ever taken," John told his sister.

Chelsea agreed, "I think it is fun, too. The zoo has many animals for us to see."

"There are six different types of monkeys at this zoo," John said. "I think they're the best animals here!"

"My favorites are the reindeer," said Chelsea. "They live where the weather is very cold."

"We learned a lot at the zoo today," said the teacher as everyone climbed on the bus to go back to school. "Tomorrow we will write stories about the things we have learned," added the teacher.

Fluency Goal: Read 115 words in one minute. The highlighted word is the 115th word in the passage. See pages 12 and 13 for information on fluency.

Meta para la fluidez: Leer 115 palabras en un minuto. La palabra destacada es la palabra número 115 en la historia. Ver las paginas 12 y 13 para más información sobre la fluidez de la lectura.

Finding Area on a Grid

Area is the space inside a figure. Find the area of each figure. Circle the correct letter.

El área es el espacio adentro de una figura. Encuentra el área de cada figura. Encierra en un círculo la letra correcta.

1. What is the area of the figure drawn on the grid?

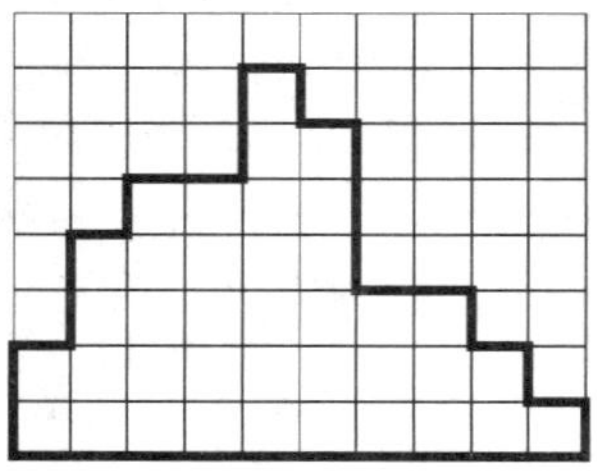

(A) 38 square units
(B) 39 square units
(C) 36 square units
(D) 41 square units

2. What is the area of the figure drawn on the grid?

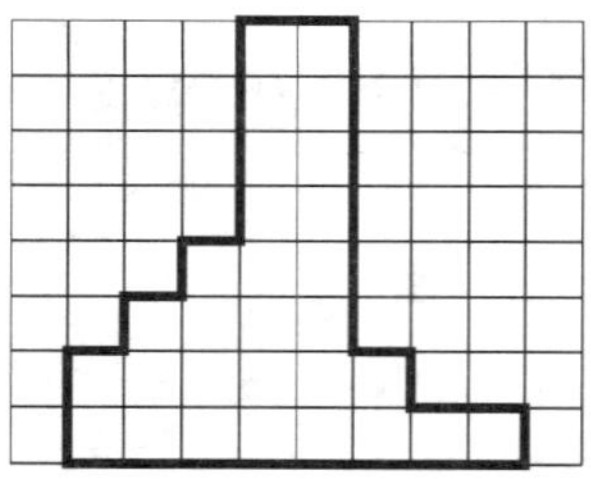

(A) 27 square units
(B) 28 square units
(C) 29 square units
(D) 32 square units

3. What is the area of the figure drawn on the grid?

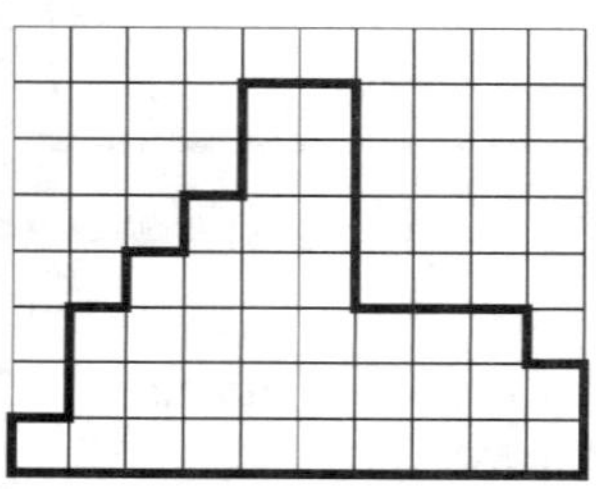

4. What is the area of the figure drawn the grid?

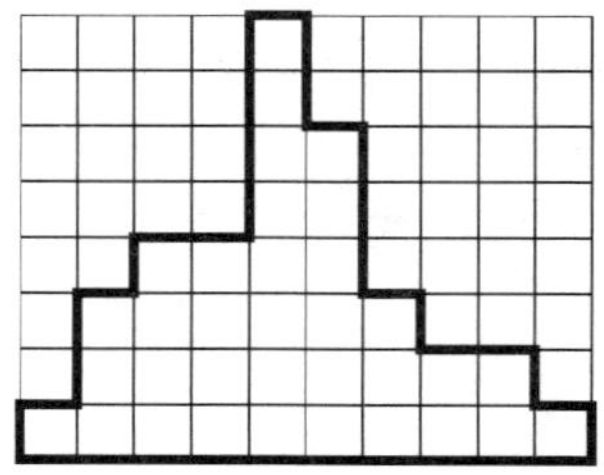

(A) 31 square units
(B) 34 square units
(C) 33 square units
(D) 36 square units

5. What is the area of the figure drawn the grid?

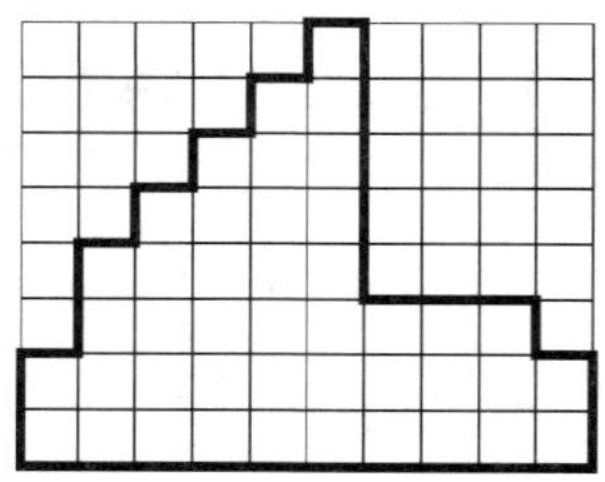

(A) 42 square units
(B) 40 square units
(C) 45 square units
(D) 43 square units

6. What is the area of the figure drawn the grid?

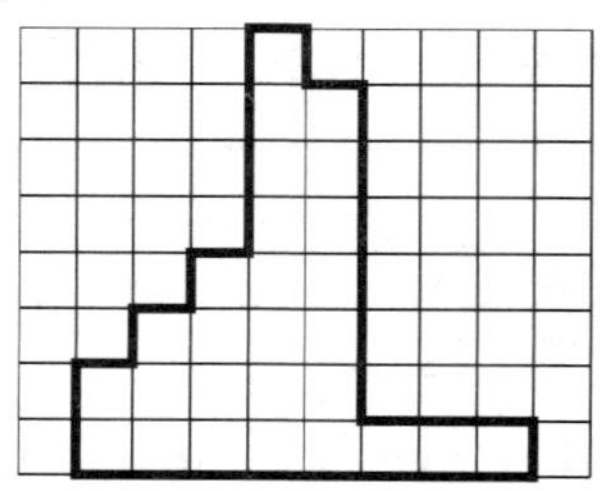

This Is the Story

One kind of paragraph is called narrative. A narrative paragraph gives the details of an experience or event in story form. It explains what happens usually in a natural time order. You have probably written a narrative paragraph before, but you just didn't know what to call it. You have definitely spoken a narrative paragraph. On the first day of school, you probably went home and told someone all about it in chronological, or time order.

Look at the writing frame below. Choose one of the main ideas in parentheses or use one of your own. Write a narrative paragraph about that idea. Put the ideas in chronological order. Use another piece of paper if you need more room.

Un tipo de párrafo es el narrativo. Un párrafo narrativo da detalles de una experiencia o acontecimiento en forma de cuento. Explica lo que sucede en una secuencia normal. Probablemente ya hayas escrito párrafos narrativos antes, pero no sabías que se llamaban así. Con seguridad, también has hablado en forma de párrafo narrativo. El primer día de clases, probablemente fuiste a casa y le contaste a alguien todo lo que pasó ese día en orden cronológico.

Mira el marco de escritura abajo. Elige una de las ideas principales entre paréntesis o usa una propia. Escribe un párrafo narrativo sobre esa idea. Pon las ideas en orden cronológico. Usa otra hoja si necesitas más espacio.

The first time I ever (*rode a bike*, *cooked*, *baby-sat)* was a total disaster.

First, ____________________

____

____

Next, ____________________

____

____

Then, ____________________

____

____

Finally, ____________________

____

____

Choose the Adjectives

Adjectives describe people, places, and things.
Los adjetivos describen gente, lugares, y cosas.

a **diamond** ring

many **loose** **funny** **large** **striped**

Use the words above to add an adjective to each sentence. Write the word on the line.

Usa las palabras anteriores para agregarle un adjetivo a cada oración. Escribe la palabra en el renglón.

1. The ____________________ zebra is a beautiful animal.
2. My clothes are baggy and ____________________.
3. ____________________ people watch television each day.
4. We laughed at the ____________________ movie.
5. The giant was so ____________________ he blocked the sun when he stood.

Add adjectives to each sentence below. Write the new sentences.

Agrégale adjetivos a cada oración siguiente. Escribe oraciones nuevas.

6. The monkeys swing from the trees.
   The silly monkeys swing from the tall, swaying palm trees.
7. The owl hooted in the night.
   ____
8. The farmer plants his crops.
   ____
9. Have you seen my shoes?
   ____
10. A hummingbird flew past the window.
    ____

Working with Money

A unit cost is the cost for one item. Find the unit cost for each item at each store. Circle the better deal.

El costo de una unidad es el costo de una sola cosa. Encuentra el costo por unidad de cada artículo de estas tiendas. Encierra en un círculo el mejor precio.

	Item	We Cost U Less	Bigger is Better	Best Unit Price
1.		1 crayon for $.80	5 crayons for $3.00 $3.00 ÷ 5 = $ .60	$ .60 each
2.		1 disk for $.10	7 disks for $2.10	________ each
3.		1 pencil for $.10	6 pencils for $1.20	________ each
4.		1 slice for $2.00	7 slices for $5.60	________ each
5.		1 bag for $3.50	2 bags for $5.00	________ each
6.		1 juicebox for $.35	5 juiceboxes for $1.25	________ each
7.		1 deck for $.70	2 decks for $.90	________ each
8.		1 book for $6.80	4 books for $40.00	________ each

When Winter Comes

Read the story and then answer the questions.

Lee el cuento y luego responde las preguntas.

What is winter like where you live? Is winter cold and snowy? If so, you probably live in the northern part of our country. For animals who live in the north, winter can be hard. How do these animals find food? How do they keep warm? How do they stay alive when winter comes?

In winter, food is hard to find. Squirrels get ready for winter by saving nuts. When nuts grow ripe, the squirrels look for all kinds of nuts. With their teeth, they cut nuts from trees and let them drop to the ground. Gray squirrels bury their nuts. The gray squirrel digs a hole with its paws. It picks up a nut with its teeth and drops it into the hole. Then it covers the nut with earth. Each squirrel buries hundreds of nuts. When winter comes, the squirrel makes a home high up in a tree. When it wants to eat, it pushes away the snow and digs up a nut. It saves enough nuts to last until spring.

Beavers also save food for winter. They save tree branches and logs. A family of beavers works together cutting down trees with their teeth and biting off the branches. They get the branches and logs to their house in the middle of the pond by dragging, carrying, pushing, or rolling them there. Then the beavers begin a food pile by anchoring the branches and logs under water near their homes. Soon the pile of wood reaches above the water. In winter, ice covers the beavers' pond and snow covers their house. When a beaver is hungry, it slips out of the house and swims under the ice. It grabs a branch from the food pile and carries it home. Then it nibbles at the bark, as though it were eating corn on the cob. That's all it eats while winter lasts.

Fluency Goal: Read 115 words in one minute. The highlighted word is the 115th word in the passage. See pages 12 and 13 for information on fluency.

***Meta para la fluidez:** Leer 115 palabras en un minuto. La palabra destacada es la palabra número 115 en el cuento. Ver las páginas 12 y 13 para más información sobre la fluidez de la lectura.*

1. When do the beavers eat the bark they have stored underwater?

- **A.** when they want to practice swimming
- **B.** during the winter
- **C.** when they don't feel like going all the way to land
- **D.** during the summer

2. In this passage, which animals bury nuts in the ground?

- **J.** all squirrels
- **K.** gray squirrels
- **L.** beavers
- **M.** red squirrels

3. You can tell that the word *anchoring* means

- **A.** floating away.
- **B.** keeping in place.
- **C.** nibbling at.
- **D.** covering with ice.

4. What is the main idea of this passage?

- **J.** Beavers swim under the ice to reach their food supply.
- **K.** Winter is cold and snowy in the northern parts of our country.
- **L.** Some animals prepare for winter by storing up food during warm weather.
- **M.** Squirrels know how to dig holes.

Multiplication Word Problems

Write a number sentence to solve these problems.

Escribe una oracíon numérica para resolver los siguientes problemas.

1. What is the product of 3 and 20? $3 \times 20 = 60$

2. How much is 3 times 48? ____________________

3. Multiply 4 by 23. ____________________

4. Joanna has 31 pennies. George has 2 times as many pennies. How many pennies does George have? ____________________

5. Jennifer collected 17 posters. Her friend, Michelle, collected 3 times as many posters. How many posters did Michelle collect? ____________________

6. What is the product of 81 and 4? ____________________

7. What is 13 times 5? ____________________

8. Daniel has 44 trading cards. James has 4 times as many cards. How many cards does James have? ____________________

9. Compute the product of 35 and 3. ____________________

10. Multiply 45 and 6. ____________________

Challenge Project for Week 4

Choose a fiction book to read. Pay close attention to the characters in the book. When you have finished reading the book, choose one of the characters that the author has helped you know well. Pretend that this character is going to be on a newscast on television. Write questions to ask this character and then write what the character's answers might be. Use another sheet of paper if you don't have enough room on this page.

When you have your script ready, get a partner. One of you will be the reporter and one will be the character. Perform your script as if you were on TV.

Escoje un libro de ficción para leer. Presta atencíon a los personajes en el libro. Cuando acabes de leer el libro, escoge uno de los personajes que el autor te haya ayudado conocer bien. Imagina que este personaje va a salir en un noticiario en la televisión. Escribe preguntas para hacerle al personaje y luego escribe las respuestas probables del personaje. Usa otra hoja de papel si no tienes suficiente lugar en esta hoja.

Cuando tengas tu guión listo, obtén un compañero. Uno de ustedes será el reportero y uno será el personaje. Interpreten su guión como si estuvieran en la televisión.

Question: ______________________________

____

____

Answer: ______________________________

____

____

Question: ______________________________

____

____

Answer: ______________________________

____

____

Question: ______________________________

____

____

Answer: ______________________________

____

____

Here Is Something to Smile About

____

(Name)

has completed the work for Week 4 of

Kids Learn!

____

(Date)

Proper Nouns

Proper nouns are the specific names of people, places, and things (including days, months, and holidays). All proper nouns must be capitalized.

Put the proper nouns from the word box in their correct columns below. Be sure to add the capital letters!

Los sustantivos propios son los nombres específicos de personas, lugares y cosas. Todos los sustantivos propios van con mayúscula (como por ejemplo días y meses en inglés, y feriados). Coloca los sustantivos propios del cuadro de palabras en la columna correcta a continuación. ¡Asegúrate de usar mayúsculas!

rocky mountains	november	alexander	christmas	monday
mr. peterson	plum street	thursday	south america	sandy
saturday	august	thanksgiving	russia	february
mardi gras	spot	fluffy	colorado river	march

Names *(people and pets)*	**Places**
	Rocky Mountains

Days	**Months**	**Holidays**

Practicing Analogies

Read the words that are being compared. Fill in each blank with the best word from the word box.

Lee las palabras que se están comparando. Completa cada espacio en blanco con la mejor palabra del cuadro de palabras.

Cat is to **pet** as **car** is to **vehicle.**

bird	**goal**	**night**	**skin**	**winter**
coloring	**head**	**quack**	**swim**	**year**

1. Chicken is to cluck as duck is to quack.
2. Banana is to peel as apple is to ____________.
3. Football is to touchdown as hockey is to ____________.
4. Bird is to fly as fish is to ____________.
5. Leaf is to tree as feather is to ____________.
6. Pencil is to write as crayon is to ____________.
7. Light is to day as dark is to ____________.
8. Day is to week as month is to ____________.
9. Hot is to summer as cold is to ____________.
10. Roof is to house as hat is to ____________.

Writing Numbers

Circle the correct answer for each expanded form problem.

Circula la respuesta correcta para cada problema ampliado de la forma.

1. Write 1,524 in expanded form.
(A) 15,000 + 200 + 40
(B) 10,000 + 5,000 + 20 + 4
(C) 1,000 + 50 + 5
(D) 1,000 + 500 + 20 + 4

2. Write 6,769 in expanded form.
(A) 67,000 + 600 + 90
(B) 6,000 + 700 + 60 + 9
(C) 60,000 + 7,000 + 60 + 9
(D) 6,000 + 70 + 7

3. Write 2,887 in expanded form.
(A) 2,000 + 80 + 8
(B) 28,000 + 800 + 70
(C) 20,000 + 8,000 + 80 + 7
(D) 2,000 + 800 + 80 + 7

4. Write 4,935 in expanded form.
(A) 4,000 + 90 + 9
(B) 49,000 + 300 + 50
(C) 40,000 + 9,000 + 30 + 5
(D) 4,000 + 900 + 30 + 5

5. Write 3,316 in expanded form.
(A) 3,000 + 30 + 3
(B) 30,000 + 3,000 + 10 + 6
(C) 33,000 + 100 + 60
(D) 3,000 + 300 + 10 + 6

6. Write 7,529 in expanded form.
(A) 7,000 + 500 + 20 + 9
(B) 7,000 + 50 + 5
(C) 75,000 + 200 + 90
(D) 70,000 + 5,000 + 20 + 9

7. Write 2,834 in expanded form.
(A) 2,000 + 800 + 30 + 4
(B) 2,000 + 80 + 8
(C) 20,000 + 8,000 + 30 + 4
(D) 28,000 + 300 + 40

8. Write 9,157 in expanded form.
(A) 91,000 + 500 + 70
(B) 90,000 + 1,000 + 50 + 7
(C) 9,000 + 100 + 50 + 7
(D) 9,000 + 10 + 1

9. Write 6,418 in expanded form.
(A) 6,000 + 40 + 4
(B) 6,000 + 400 + 10 + 8
(C) 60,000 + 4,000 + 10 + 8
(D) 64,000 + 100 + 80

10. Write 2,537 in expanded form.
(A) 25,000 + 300 + 70
(B) 2,000 + 500 + 30 + 7
(C) 20,000 + 5,000 + 30 + 7
(D) 2,000 + 50 + 5

First Person Voice

Read the entry in the diary below. The author, Ashley, recorded her thoughts and feelings. She used the words *I* and *me* often. When she reads her diary again, she will know that she means herself when she reads those pronouns. When you read something with the words *I* or *me*, meaning the author, it is written in what is called the **voice of the first person**. The diary is written in the voice of the first person.

Lee los apuntes en el siguiente diario. La autora, Ashley, registró sus pensamientos y sentimientos. Usó las palabras I y me muchas veces. Cuando leas el diario de nuevo, sabrás que se refiere a sí misma al leer esos pronombres. Cuando lees algo con las palabras I o me, que se refieren al autor, decimos que está escrito en lo que se llama la voz de la primera persona. El diario está escrito en primera persona.

Dear Diary,

I wonder how the animals in the zoo feel when the weather is this cold. I worry that their fur and feathers will not keep them warm enough. It bothers me to think that the animals may be cold. Tomorrow, I will ask my teacher about how animals keep warm.

Ashley

Put a check after the sentences below that are written in the first person.

Pon una palomita después de las siguientes oraciones que están escritas en primera persona.

1. I am happy about our trip to the zoo. ____________
2. The three girls watched the polar bear dance. ____________
3. The zookeeper let me hold the owl. ____________
4. I could feel the smooth skin of the snake. ____________
5. The old monkey fussed at the younger ones. ____________

Past and Present

Verbs in the **present tense** show action that is happening now. In the **past tense**, verbs show action that already happened.

Los verbos en presente indican acción que está sucediendo en éste momento. En el pasado, los verbos indican acción que ya sucedió.

Today the bird **chirps.**

Yesterday the bird **chirped.**

Change each of these present-tense verbs to the past tense by adding *d* or *ed*.

Cambia cada uno de estos verbos en tiempo presente al tiempo pasado agregando d o ed.

1. walk walked
2. climb ______
3. jump ______
4. play ______
5. comb ______
6. roar ______
7. smile ______
8. fold ______
9. close ______
10. paint ______

Change each of the past-tense verbs to the present tense by removing the *d* or *ed*.

Cambia cada uno de estos verbos en tiempo pasado al tiempo presente quitando d o ed.

11. colored color
12. scribbled ______
13. turned ______
14. cooked ______
15. washed ______
16. shared ______
17. stacked ______
18. typed ______
19. laughed ______
20. delivered ______

Louis Braille's Code

(Born January 4, 1809)

Louis Braille was a Frenchman who invented a raised dot writing system for the blind. A special typewriter presses against paper to form the different dot sequences. Use the Braille letter dot code to write and read the messages.

Louis Braille fue un hombre francés que inventó el sistema de lecto-escritura táctil de puntos para los ciegos. Una máquina de escribir especial se prensa contra una hoja de papel para formar puntos de diferentes secuencias. Usa el código de Braille para escribir y leer mensajes.

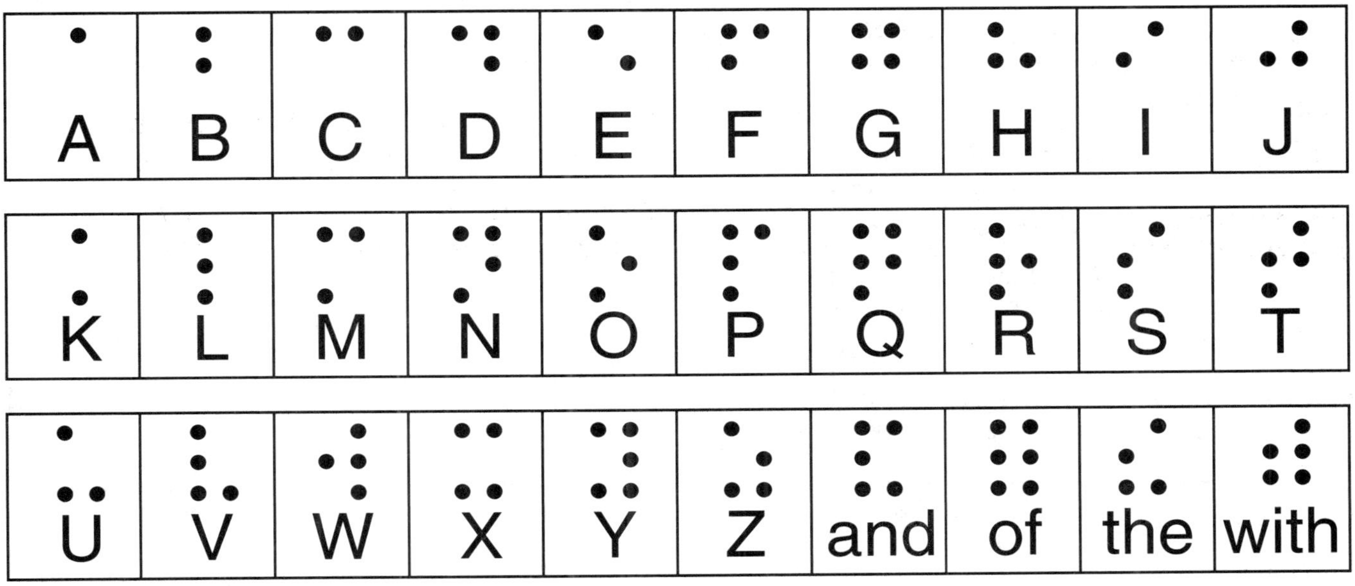

1. M ____ ____ ____ ____ ____ ____ ____ ____________.
(Fill in blank)

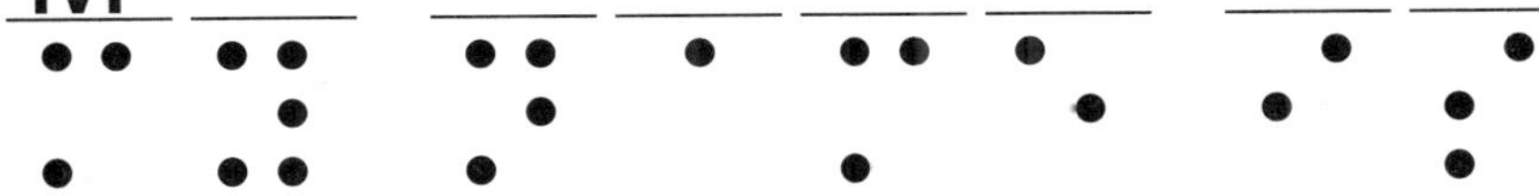

2. ____ ____ ____ ____ ____ ____ ____ ____ ____ ____ ____ ____.
(Number)

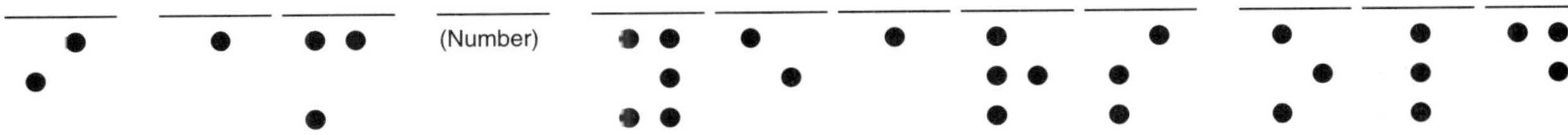

3. Challenge: Write a message in Braille dots below. Now have a friend tell you what it says!

Reto: Escribe un mensaje en puntos de Braille a continuación. ¡Ahora haz que un compañero te diga lo que dice!

Baby Animals

Read the story. Cross out the extra details. Rewrite the remaining sentences to make a summary.

Lee la historia. Tacha los detalles adicionales. Vuelve a escribir las oraciones que quedan para hacer un resumen.

Every animal has babies. Sometimes the mother takes care of the baby until it can take care of itself. Baby animals are cute. Sometimes a whole group of animals cares for the babies. Baby bears are called cubs. Cubs like to eat honey. Some bears like to eat fish and nuts, too. Baby animals must eat. Mothers and fathers protect their babies. The babies are small and cannot find food for themselves. Some baby animals, like kangaroos, live in pouches. Baby kangaroos are called joeys. They will live in their mother's pouch for nine months. Other baby animals travel on their mothers' backs. Possums and monkeys carry babies on their backs. Baby animals are fun to watch.

Fluency Goal: Read 115 words in one minute. The highlighted word is the 115th word in the passage. See pages 12 and 13 for information on fluency.

***Meta para la fluidez:** Leer 115 palabras en un minuto. La palabra destacada es la palabra número 115 en la historia.* *Ver las páginas 12 y 13 para más información sobre la fluidez de la lectura.*

Summary

Division Tables

Follow the rule at the top of each table. Complete each table.

Sigue la regla al comienzo de cada tabla. Termina cada tabla.

Example: ÷ 2	
4	2
2	1
6	3
8	4

1.

÷ 3	
9	
6	
15	
12	

2.

÷ 6	
12	
6	
24	
18	

3.

÷ 8	
8	
48	
24	
40	

4.

÷ 4	
16	
8	
40	
32	

5.

÷ 7	
49	
35	
70	
14	

6.

÷ 9	
36	
90	
45	
81	

7.

÷ 5	
15	
25	
35	
50	

Write the correct divisor for each table.

Escribe el divisor correcto para cada tabla.

8.

÷ ______	
10	0
3	0
6	0

9.

÷ ______	
7	7
4	4
1	1

10.

÷ ______	
6	1
60	10
36	6

11.

÷ ______	
70	10
35	5
14	2

Jazz it Up!

Rewrite the paragraphs below. Add some descriptive words. You may use the Word Box below to help you.

Vuelve a escribir los párrafos siguientes. Agrega algunas palabras descriptivas. Puedes usar el cuadro de palabras como ayuda.

Sleeping with the Dinosaurs at the Museum

When it was time to set up our "camp," I knew just what to do. I decided we would bed down under the apatosaurus. Its ribcage overhead would look cool in the beam of my flashlight.

People were scattered on the floor around us. The sounds of voices echoed in the halls. Moonlight streamed in through a window.

Word Box

- enormous
- towering
- long
- sleepy
- grand
- content
- bright

Which Is It?

Read the number sentences. Add the correct math sign to each problem to make the number sentence true.

Lee las oraciones numéricas. Agrega el signo matemático correcto a cada problema para que la oración sea verdadera.

+	-	×	÷
add	subtract	multiply	divide

1. 5 [+] 7 = 12
2. 24 [ ] 4 = 6
3. 9 [ ] 3 = 12
4. 18 [ ] 6 = 12
5. 4 [ ] 9 = 13
6. 4 [ ] 9 = 36
7. 10 [ ] 8 = 80
8. 15 [ ] 5 = 3
9. 11 [ ] 4 = 7
10. 8 [ ] 16 = 24
11. 2 [ ] 8 = 16
12. 3 [ ] 2 = 5
13. 22 [ ] 6 = 16
14. 9 [ ] 1 = 10
15. 3 [ ] 3 = 9

Challenge Project for Week 5

Choose a book. If you do not have one at home, check one out from the library. Write a book review.

Elige un libro. Si no tienes ninguno en tu casa, saca uno de la biblioteca. Escribe una reseña del libro.

A Review of ______________________________

1. What I liked best about this book was ______________ because ______________________________

   ____
2. Another thing I liked was ______________ because ______________________________

   ____
3. What I did not like about this book was ______________ because ______________________________

   ____
4. The best character was ______________ because ______________________________

   ____
5. I think the book would be better if ______________

   ____

   ____
6. One part I would not change is ______________

   ____

   ____
7. The person I think would enjoy this book is ______________

   ____

You're a Star!

____

(Name)

has completed
Week 5 of
Kids Learn!

____

(Date)

Order the Words

List these words in alphabetical order.

Ordena estas palabras alfabéticamente.

river	friend	vest	jump
moon	house	silent	light
cart	ghost	tunnel	umbrella

cart ____________ ____________

____________ ____________ ____________

____________ ____________ ____________

____________ ____________ ____________

List these words in alphabetical order. You will need to look at the second letters as well as the first.

Ordena estas palabras alfabéticamente. Tendrás que fijarte en las letras segundas así como en las primeras.

dog	game	same	science
sort	lunch	grass	cell
loop	cane	lion	deer

____________ ____________ ____________

____________ ____________ ____________

____________ ____________ ____________

____________ ____________ ____________

Word Problems

Choose the operation needed to solve each problem. Then solve the problem.

Elige la operación que se necesita para resolver cada problema. Resuelve el problema.

1. One box of cereal has 18 servings. How many servings in 22 boxes?

   \+ − x ÷

   18 x 22 = 396

2. Jason had \$25.00. He spent \$12.93 buying a new CD. How much money does he have left?

   \+ − x ÷

3. There is a total of 50 coins in 10 rolls. How many coins are in each roll?

   \+ − x ÷

4. Amy caught 18 fish. James caught 6 fewer fish than Amy. How many fish did James catch?

   \+ − x ÷

5. There is a total of 60 hens in 10 hen houses. How many hens in each house?

   \+ − x ÷

6. Each van can carry 9 people. How many people can 4 vans carry?

   \+ − x ÷

7. Josh counted 30 cars. Sybil counted 7 more cars than Josh. How many cars did Sybil count?

   \+ − x ÷

8. There is a total of 6 flags. Each flag has 50 stars. How many stars in all?

   \+ − x ÷

9. There is a total of 32 paper clips in 4 boxes. How many paper clips in each box?

   \+ − x ÷

10. Yesterday it was 97° F. Today it is only 80° F. What is the difference in temperature?

    \+ − x ÷

My Dream

Read the story and then answer the questions.

Lee la historia y luego responde a las preguntas.

I had a dream last night that I was five inches tall. In my dream, I climbed down my bedpost and onto the floor. I walked right under my bed and across the room. It was a good thing my mom wasn't in the dream because if she had seen everything stuffed under my bed, she would have made me clean my room! Instead, I walked over to my dollhouse and through the front door. Everything was just my size! I arranged all the furniture for a party, and I invited all my dolls to come over. We danced around the dollhouse, told jokes, and ate the cookies on my nightstand, left over from my bedtime snack. We had such a great time, I decided to live in the dollhouse forever. I went upstairs to the doll bedroom, and stretching out on the tiny bed, I fell asleep.

When I woke up from my dream, I smiled as I remembered it. Then I looked inside my dollhouse and wondered, "How did those cookie crumbs get in there?"

Fluency Goal: Read 115 words in one minute. The highlighted word is the 115th word in the passage. See pages 12 and 13 for information on fluency.

***Meta para la fluidez:** Leer 115 palabras en un minuto. La palabra destacada es la palabra número 115 en la historia.* *Ver las páginas 12 y 13 para más información sobre la fluidez de la lectura.*

1. How did the girl get down from her bed? ______________________

____

2. What was the girl glad her mother did not see? ______________________

____

3. What did the girl do to get ready for the party? ______________________

____

4. What did the partygoers eat? ______________________

____

5. What surprised the girl when she woke from her dream? ______________________

____

More Thesaurus Practice

Here is an entry from a thesaurus. Use it to answer the questions.

Aquí está una entrada de un tesauro. Úsala para contestar las siguientes preguntas.

> **show:** *n.* 1. performance, presentation, act
>
> **show:** *v.* 1. reveal, display, teach, instruct
> 2. *Ant.* hide (from), cover up

1. You can infer from this thesaurus entry that a show
   A. is meant to hide things.
   B. is what happens in real life.
   C. is a type of classroom.
   D. entertains people

Read this sentence.

Lee esta oración.

> The girl needed someone to show her how to multiply.

2. Which *synonym* (same) could be used to replace the word show in the sentence?
   A. teach
   B. ask
   C. reveal
   D. display

Read this sentence.

Lee esta oración.

> Every Friday students get to bring something from home to show to the class.

3. Which *antonym* (opposite) could be used to replace the word show in the sentence?
   A. display
   B. hide from
   C. cover
   D. perform

Tell the Place

Write the place value (ones, tens, hundreds, or thousands) of the circled number.

Escribe el valor (unidades, decenas, centenas o millares) del número que está encerrado en el círculo.

1. 7,710 thousands

2. 5,188 ____________

3. 9,877 ____________

4. 4,820 ____________

5. 8,253 ____________

6. 2,691 ____________

7. 3,269 ____________

8. 1,498 ____________

9. 6,260 ____________

10. 3,134 ____________

Circle the largest digit. Write its place value.

Encierra en un círculo el dígito más grande. Escribe su valor.

11. 1,480 tens

12. 1,401 ____________

13. 7,653 ____________

14. 6,581 ____________

15. 3,481 ____________

16. 9,326 ____________

17. 7,363 ____________

18. 5,984 ____________

19. 8,601 ____________

20. 7,181 ____________

Using each set of numbers, make both the largest number possible and the smallest number possible. (Note: Zero cannot be used in the thousands place.)

Con cada conjunto de números, forma el número más grande posible y el número más pequeño posible. (Nota: El cero no se puede usar en el lugar de los millares.)

	Largest Number	**Smallest Number**
21. (2, 1, 5, 0)	5,210	1,025
22. (3, 3, 4, 2)		
23. (3, 7, 0, 6)		
24. (6, 5, 3, 6)		
25. (5, 7, 2, 2)		
26. (6, 4, 4, 8)		
27. (5, 1, 2, 4)		
28. (6, 8, 7, 9)		

How About a Little Help?

A topic sentence does not work alone to explain the main idea of a paragraph. Helping sentences, also known as body sentences or supporting sentences, work to help the topic sentence. They help make the main idea clear.

There are three topics listed on this page. In the word bank below, find the helping or supporting details for each main idea topic. List them on the first line below each topic. Then write a paragraph for each one. The main idea would be included in your topic sentence. The helping ideas would be included in your body sentences.

Una oración temática sola no explica la idea principal de un párrafo. Otras oraciones, conocidas como auxiliares o secundarias, la respaldan. Estas oraciones ayudan a que la idea principal sea clara.

Hay tres ideas principales en esta página. En el banco de palabras a continuación, encuentra ideas auxiliares o secundarias para cada idea principal. La idea principal se debe incluir en la oración temática. Las ideas secundarias se deben incluir en las oraciones auxiliares.

Word Bank				
tires	refrigerators	knees	frying pans	bumpers
ears	ovens	steering wheels	thumbs	

1. Main Idea: **car parts**

   Supporting Ideas: ______________________________

   ____

   ____

   ____

2. Main Idea: **kitchen things**

   Supporting Ideas: ______________________________

   ____

   ____

   ____

3. Main Idea: **body parts**

   Supporting Ideas: ______________________________

   ____

   ____

   ____

Running Rivers

Use the numbers 1–10 to rank the rivers in order from **longest** to **shortest**.

Clasifica los ríos del más largo al más corto con números del 1 al 10.

Rank	River	Length	Rank	River	Length
______	Arkansas	1,396 miles	______	Red	1,018 miles
______	Columbia	1,210 miles	______	Rio Grande	1,885 miles
______	Mississippi	2,348 miles	______	St. Lawrence	760 miles
______	Missouri	2,315 miles	______	Snake	1,083 miles
______	Ohio	981 miles	______	Yukon	1,979 miles

1. Which river is longer than the Missouri River? ______________________
2. Which river is shorter than the Ohio River? ______________________
3. Which river is longer than the Columbia River and shorter than the Rio Grande?

   ____

4. Which river is longer than the Red River and shorter than the Columbia River?

   ____

5. How many rivers are longer than 1,500 miles? ______________________
6. How many rivers are longer than 1,000 miles but less than 1,500 miles? __________
7. How many rivers are shorter than 1,000 miles? __________

Use the lengths of each river to write and solve each math problem.

8. Arkansas + Yukon + Snake = ________
9. Mississippi + Red + Ohio = ________
10. Missouri – Yukon = ________
11. Columbia – St. Lawrence = ________

Sentence Types and Their End Marks

Put a period, a question mark, or an exclamation mark at the end of each sentence below. On the line after the sentence, write **declarative**, **interrogative**, **imperative**, or **exclamatory**.

Coloca un punto, un signo de pregunta o un signo de exclamación al final de cada una de las siguientes oraciones. En el renglón después de la oración, escribe si es enunciativa, interrogativa, imperativa o exclamativa.

1. Oh, boy, it's time for recess! exclamatory
2. I'm not sure where to go because I'm new here __________
3. Where do I go for recess __________
4. Do you mean way over there where it's all sandy __________
5. Oh, well, at least there are some swings over here __________
6. Hey, watch where you're going __________
7. Don't throw sand __________
8. Now that's an interesting looking ball __________
9. Where did you get it __________
10. Be careful where you throw that thing __________
11. Can I play, too __________
12. I'm not kidding; I really like to play __________
13. Oh, no, there goes the bell __________
14. Okay, class, let's line up __________
15. Did everyone have fun during recess __________

All Together Now

Each set of words belongs to a different group. Classify the group by writing its group name on the line.

Cada conjunto de palabras corresponde a un grupo distinto. Clasifica el grupo escribiendo el nombre del grupo en el renglón.

1. Oak, maple, and pine are ______trees______.
2. Kenneth, Brent, and Ryan are ____________.
3. Main, Elm, and First are ____________.
4. London, Paris, and Los Angeles are ____________.
5. Ladybug, fly, and grasshopper are ____________.
6. *The Cat in the Hat, Charlotte's Web,* and *Goodnight Moon* are ____________.
7. Happy, sad, and angry are ____________.
8. Norway, China, and Peru are ____________.
9. Doll, top, and blocks are ____________.
10. Jeans, sweatshirt, and pajamas are ____________.
11. Pacific, Atlantic, and Indian are ____________.
12. Sandals, loafers, and slippers are ____________.
13. Corn, broccoli, and asparagus are ____________.
14. Turkey, pastrami, and peanut butter and jelly are ____________.
15. Baseball, football, and hockey are ____________.

Identifying Solids

Circle the correct letter.

Encierra en un círculo la letra correcta.

1. Which solid do dice look like?

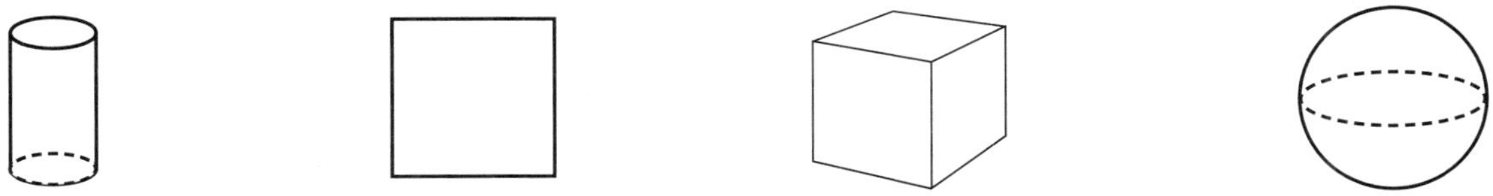

(A) cylinder (B) square (C) cube (D) sphere

2. Which solid does a stick of butter look like?

(A) cube (B) cylinder (C) rectangular prism (D) square

3. Which solid does a basketball look like?

(A) cone (B) pyramid (C) cylinder (D) sphere

4. What solid does a party hat look like?

(A) cube (B) cylinder (C) sphere (D) cone

5. What solid does a tennis ball can look like?

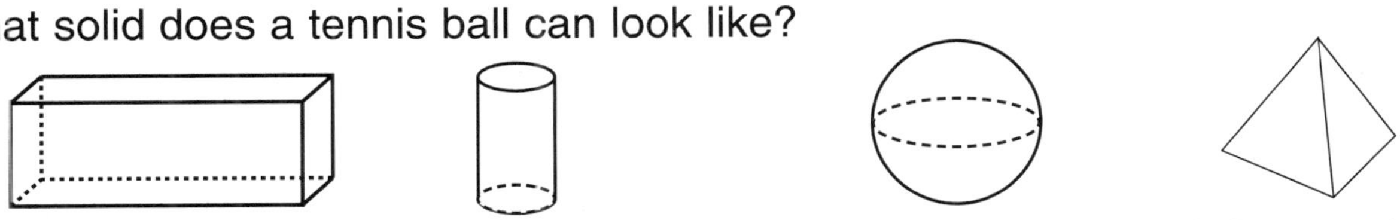

(A) rectangular prism (B) cylinder (C) sphere (D) pyramid

Challenge Project for Week 6

Directions: Have you ever had a mouse, rat, or hamster for a pet? Rodents can make great pets. For this activity, you will pretend to buy a pet mouse. Your job is to research about all the necessary equipment, food, toys, and whatever else is needed to make your mouse happy and healthy. Write a short paragraph about what you have learned.

***Instrucciones:** ¿Alguna vez tuviste un ratón, una rata o un hámster como mascota? Los roedores pueden ser mascotas excelentes. Para esta actividad, vamos a suponer que compraste un ratón. Tu trabajo es investigar todo el equipo necesario, alimento, juguetes y cualquier cosa que se necesite para que tu ratón esté feliz y sano. Escribe un párrafo breve de lo que has aprendido.*

Picture This!

____

(Name)

has completed the work in Week 6 of Kids Learn!

____

(Date)

Cursive Alphabet

Trace these letters to practice cursive writing.

Traza estas letras para practicar las letras en cursiva.

Aa Bb

Cc Dd

Ee Ff

Gg Hh

Ii Jj

Kk Ll

Mm

Cursive Alphabet *(cont.)*

Trace these letters to practice cursive writing.

Traza estas letras para practicar las letras en cursiva.

Nn Oo

Pp Qq

Rr Ss

Tt Uu

Vv Ww

Xx Yy

Zz

Number Lines with Equivalent Fractions

Use these number lines to help you understand equivalent fractions.

Usa estas rectas numéricas para entender las fracciones equivalentes.

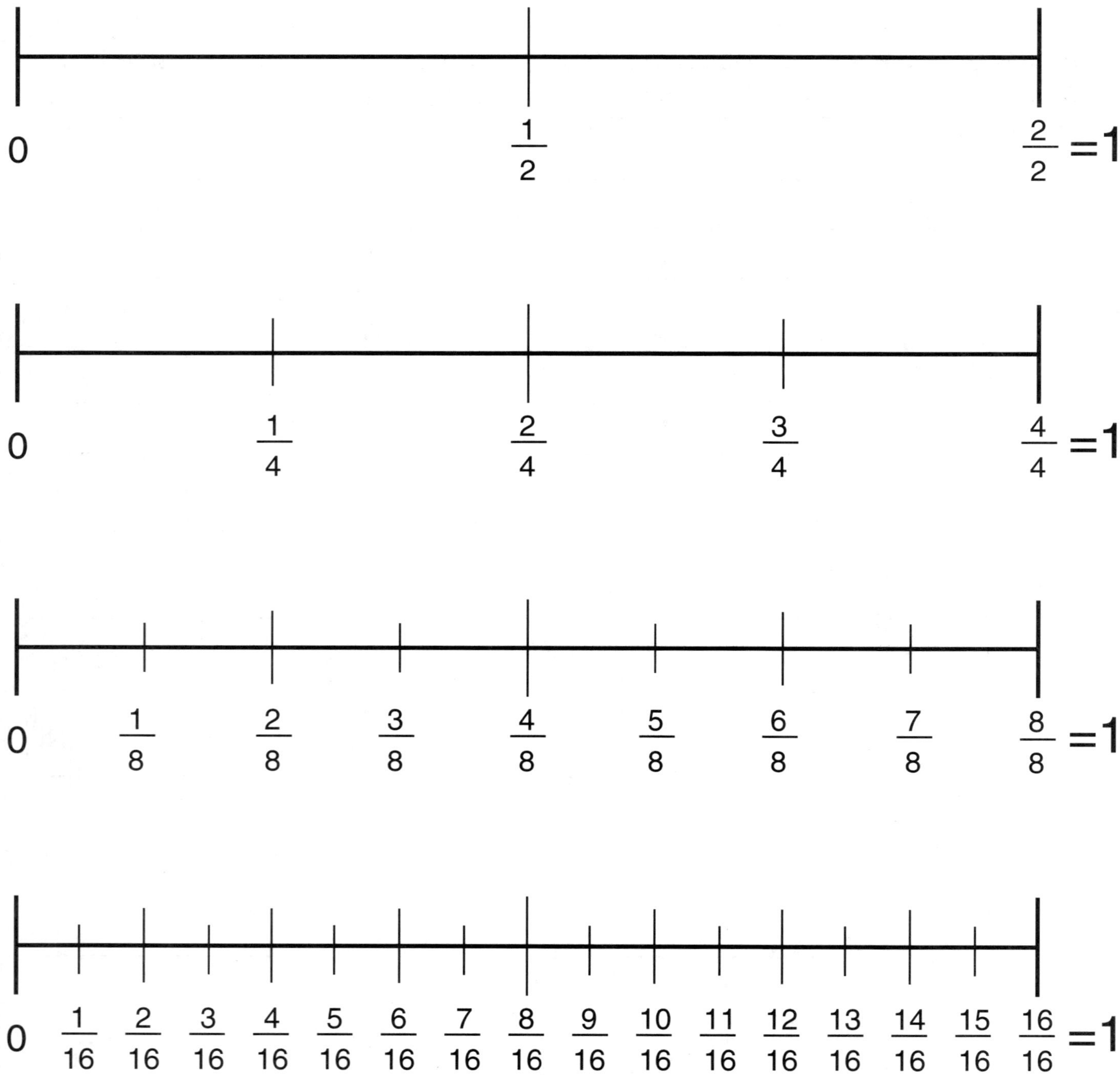

Book Wheel

Place a paper clip on the dot at the center of the Book Wheel. Place the tip of a pencil on the dot. Spin the paper clip around the pencil. Read a book from the section to which the arrow points. Write the name of the book in the section, then spin again! Be sure to read at least one book from each section.

Coloca un clip en el punto del centro de la rueda de libros. Coloca la punta de un lápiz en el punto. Gira el clip alrededor del lápiz. Lee un libro de la sección que señala la flecha. Escribe el nombre del libro en la sección, y luego ¡gira de nuevo! Asegúrate de leer por lo menos un libro de cada sección.

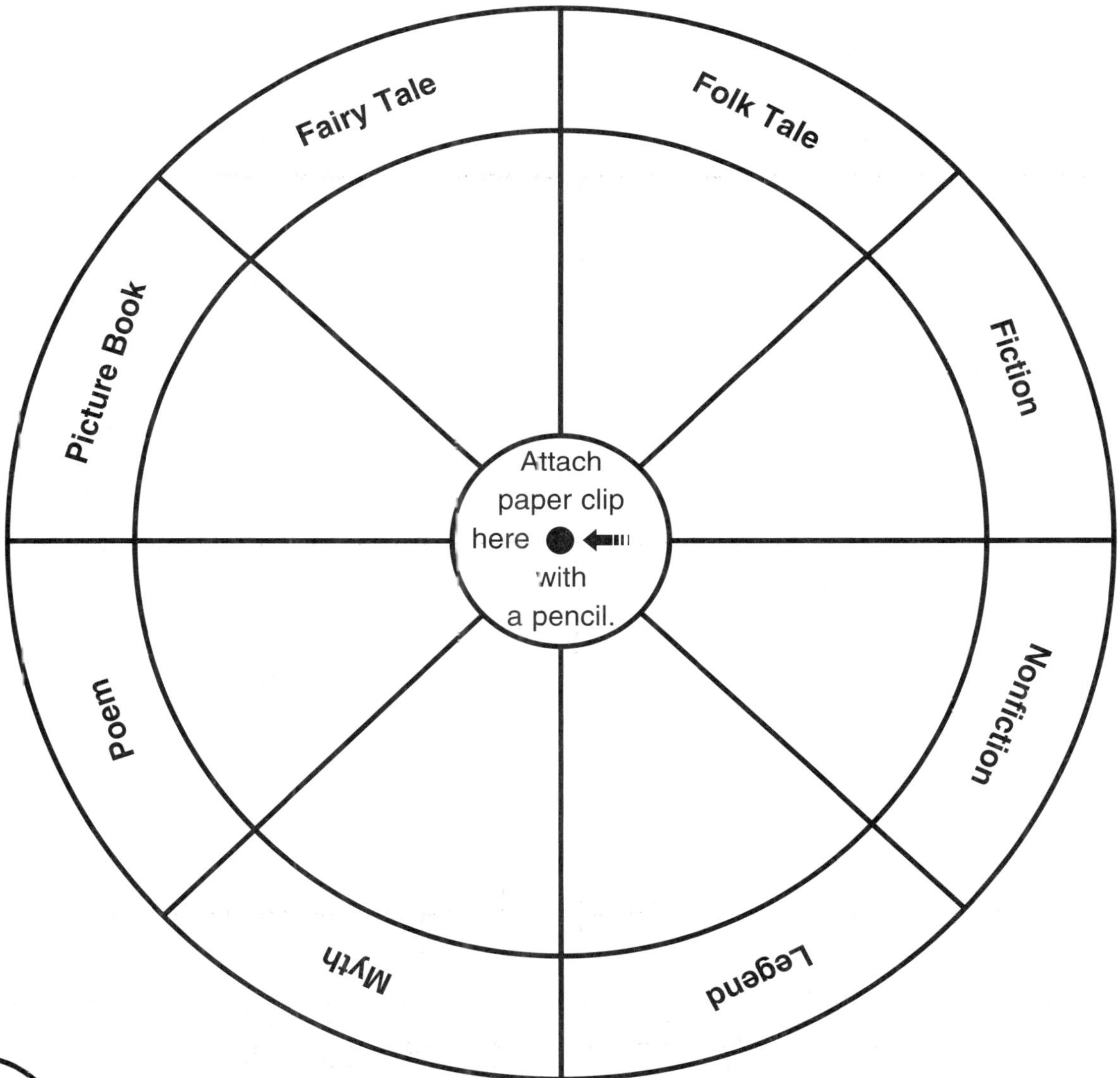

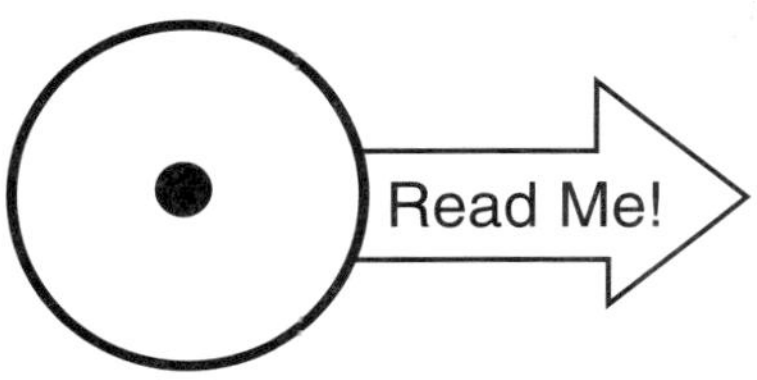

(This page is left blank so you can cut out the manipulatives on the previous page.)

(Esta página está en blanco para permitirle cortar los manipulativos de la página anterior.)

Answer Key

Page 20

There are many possibilities. The following are some ideas:

–an: ran, pan, ban, can, fan

–ark: bark, dark, hark, lark, mark

–eat: beat, feat, heat, meat, neat

–ame: came, dame, fame, game, lame

–ear: bear, dear, fear, gear, near

–our: four, hour, pour, sour

–ine: dine, fine, line, mine, pine

–ice: dice, mice, nice, rice

–up: cup, pup, sup

Page 21

1. spring, summer, autumn, winter
2. one time

Page 22

1. <, less
2. >, greater
3. >, greater
4. <, less
5. <, less
6. >, greater
7. <, less
8. <, less
9. <, less
10. <, less
11. >, greater
12. >, greater
13. <, less
14. <, less
15. <, less
16. >, greater
17. <, less

Page 23

1. excited
2. sad
3. silly
4. worried
5. happy

Page 24

Subject and predicate choices will vary.

1. S
2. S
3. P
4. S
5. P
6. S
7. P
8. P
9. P
10. S

Page 25

1. $2.27
2. $2.64
3. $1.02
4. $1.57
5. $0.61
6. $0.57
7. $0.41
8. $1.48

Page 26

1. rooster
2. movie
3. computer
4. rose
5. guitar or violin

Page 27

1. D
2. A
3. B
4. C
5. A
6. C

Page 29

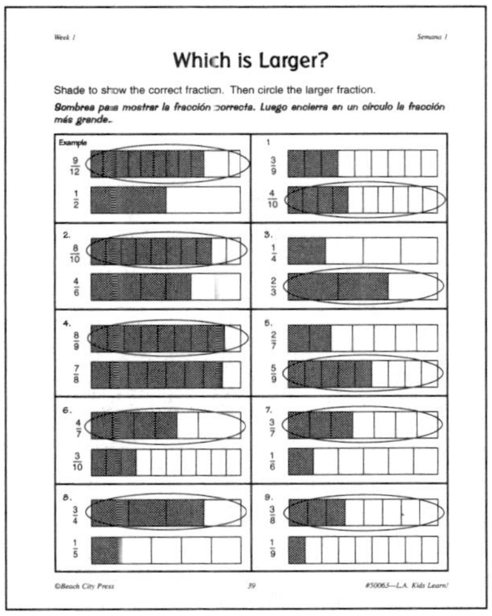

Page 32

1. Pacific Ocean
2. Grand Canyon
3. Mt. Rushmore
4. Amazon River
5. San Diego Zoo
6. Hyde Park
7. Sahara Desert
8. Lake Louise
9. Disneyland
10. North Pole
11. Rocky Mountains
12. Niagara Falls

Page 33

1. 90
2. 20
3. 70
4. 10
5. 10
6. 70
7. 80
8. 10
9. 10
10. 20
11. 20
12. 10
13. 200
14. 500
15. 100
16. 300
17. 900
18. 600
19. 400
20. 900
21. 800
22. 300
23. 200
24. 400
25. 6,000
26. 7,000
27. 1,000
28. 1,000
29. 2,000
30. 6,000
31. 7,000
32. 9,000
33. 8,000
34. 4,000
35. 2,000
36. 3,000

Page 34

1. b
2. details: don't die from disease; not killed by bugs or fungi; bark regrows after forest fire or lightning strike; when blown down, send up new shoots; when cut down, stump will send up new shoots

Page 35

1. 40 + 20 = 60; About 60 children were invited to the party.
2. 150 + 130 + 210 = 490; Mariah bought about 490 items in all.
3. 190 – 90 = 100; About 100 people said "no."
4. 210 + 320 + 60 = 590; Lucy set out about 590 jellybeans.
5. 570 – 240 = 330 – 200 = 130; The third cupcake had about 130 sprinkles.
6. 220 + 300 + 370 = 890; About 890 points were scored in all.

Page 36

1. a
2. an
3. a
4. an
5. a
6. a
7. an
8. an
9. a
10. a
11. An
12. a
13. a
14. An
15. A

Page 38

1. $1.96
2. $1.32
3. $2.25
4. $2.46

Answer Key *(cont.)*

Page 40

wood: oak, pencil, board, forest, walnut, lumber, maple

metals: tin, iron, nail, aluminum, steel, copper, bronze

water: bay, sea, pond, lake, river, ocean, creek

space: countdown, Mars, moon, orbit, astronaut, weightless, rocket

colors: tan, red, blue, green, scarlet, beige, chartreuse

furniture: lamp, couch, mirror, chest, rocker, dresser, cabinet

Page 41

1. <
2. >
3. <
4. <
5. <
6. <
7. >
8. >
9. <
10. <
11. >
12. <

Page 44

Dear Pen Pal,

I love to go to the circus! On May 6, 1999, the circus came to my hometown of Jackson, Wyoming. A parade marched through our streets, and soon the big top could be seen. Ken, my best friend, and I went to watch the performers prepare for opening night. We saw clowns, acrobats, and even the ringmaster. What a sight! Have you ever seen anything like it? You should go if you ever get the chance.

I also really enjoy playing baseball. My favorite team is the New York Yankees, but I also like the St. Louis Cardinals. When I grow up, I want to be a baseball pitcher, first baseman, or shortstop. Do you like baseball? What do you want to do when you grow up? I wish you could see my cool baseball card collection, but Ken's collection is even better.

Oh, I almost forgot to tell you about my family! There are four people in my family. They are my mom, my dad, my brother, and me. Scruffy, my cat, is also a family member. In August 2000, my grandpa will probably move in with us. I can't wait for that! Didn't you say your grandma lives with you? I'll bet you really like that.

Well, that's all for now. Please write back to me soon. See you!

Your pal,

Brent

Page 45

1. 2, 1/2 of $1.00
2. 4, 1/4 of $1.00
3. 10, 1/10 of $1.00
4. 20, 1/20 of $1.00
5. 100, 1/100 of $1.00
6. $4.83
7. $39.76
8. $281.10
9. 61/100 or $.61
10. 65/100 or $.65
11. 115/100 or $1.15
12. 85/100 or $.85

Page 46

1. A
2. B
3. D

Page 47

1. two
2. Tracy and his father
3. Tracy
4. "He" in the first sentence

Page 48

1. 90°
2. > 90°
3. < 90°
4. first triangle
5. last triangle
6. middle triangle
7. isosceles
8. scalene
9. equilateral

Page 49

Accept any reasonable topic sentence. Here are some ideas:

There are so many things to see at the zoo.

If you want to get good grades, you will need to take certain steps.

Fire can be our friend, but often it can be a dangerous destroyer.

Page 50

1. appear
2. open
3. spell
4. thank
5. good
6. clue
7. hope
8. health
9. imagine

Page 51

1. 28
2. 662
3. 8,488
4. 963
5. 848
6. 6,824
7. 939
8. 882
9. 6,284
10. 8,844
11. 648
12. 6,996
13. 3,966
14. 2,482
15. 8,246

Mystery question and answer: WHO CAN MULTIPLY? I CAN!

Page 52

Complete sentences: 2, 3, 5, 7, 9, 10, 14, 15

Page 53

The specific sections shaded may vary.

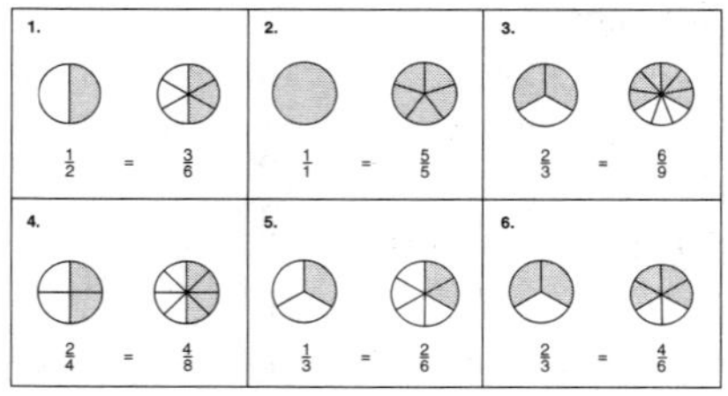

7. <
8. >
9. =
10. =
11. >
12. <

Page 56

1. can't
2. he's
3. won't
4. doesn't
5. they're
6. we're
7. shouldn't
8. it'll
9. she will
10. it is
11. must not
12. you are
13. they will
14. have not
15. I will
16. I am

Page 57

1. pail
2. Two
3. hear
4. wear
5. sew
6. high
7. wood
8. bee
9. blew
10. knew

Page 58

1. A
2. B
3. A
4. C
5. C
6. C
7. B
8. D
9. B
10. A

Answer Key *(cont.)*

Page 59

***opinions** (green)*

I think panthers are beautiful.

They are scary.

A panther would be a great pet.

No it wouldn't.

This is the best trip we have ever taken.

I think it is fun, too.

I think they're the best animals here!

My favorite is the reindeer.

We learned a lot at the zoo today.

***facts** (red)*

Panthers belong to the cat family.

They weigh more than 100 pounds.

It is against the law to keep a wild animal as a pet.

The zoo has many animals for us to see.

There are six different types of monkeys at the zoo.

They live where the weather is very cold.

Tomorrow we will write stories about the things we have learned.

Page 60

1. A
2. C
3. B
4. B
5. D
6. A

Page 62

1. striped
2. loose
3. Many
4. funny
5. large

6.–10. Answers will vary.

Page 63

1. $.60
2. $.10
3. $.10
4. $.80
5. $2.50
6. $.25
7. $.45
8. $6.80

Page 64

1. B
2. K
3. B
4. L

Page 65

1. 3 x 20 = 60
2. 3 x 48 = 144
3. 4 x 23 = 92
4. 2 x 31 = 62 pennies
5. 3 x 17 = 51 posters
6. 81 x 4 = 324
7. 13 x 5 = 65
8. 44 x 4 = 176 cards
9. 35 x 3 = 105
10. 45 x 6 = 270

Page 68

names (people and pets): Alexander, Mr. Peterson, Sandy, Spot, Fluffy

places: Rocky Mountains, Colorado River, Plum Street, Russia, South America

days: Monday, Thursday, Saturday

months: November, August, March, February

holidays: Christmas, Thanksgiving, Mardi Gras

Page 69

1. quack
2. skin
3. goal
4. swim
5. bird
6. coloring
7. night
8. year
9. winter
10. head

Page 70

1. D
2. B
3. D
4. D
5. D
6. A
7. A
8. C
9. B
10. B

Page 71

1. check
2. no check
3. check
4. check
5. no check

Page 72

1. walked
2. climbed
3. jumped
4. played
5. combed
6. roared
7. smiled
8. folded
9. closed
10. painted
11. color
12. scribble
13. turn
14. cook
15. wash
16. share
17. stack
18. type
19. laugh
20. deliver

Page 73

1. My name is ________.
2. I am _____ years old.

Page 75

1. 3, 2, 5, 4
2. 2, 1, 4, 3
3. 1, 6, 3, 5
4. 4, 2, 10, 8
5. 7, 5, 10, 2
6. 4, 10, 5, 9
7. 3, 5, 7, 10
8. 0
9. 1
10. 6
11. 7

Page 77

1. 5 + 7 = 12
2. 24 ÷ 4 = 6
3. 9 + 3 = 12
4. 18 – 6 = 12
5. 4 + 9 = 13
6. 4 x 9 = 36
7. 10 x 8 = 80
8. 15 ÷ 5 = 3
9. 11 – 4 = 7
10. 8 + 16 = 24
11. 2 x 8 = 16
12. 3 + 2 = 5
13. 22 – 6 = 16
14. 9 + 1 = 10
15. 3 x 3 = 9

Page 80

cart, friend, ghost, house, jump, light, moon, river, silent, tunnel, umbrella, vest

cane, cell, deer, dog, game, grass, lion, loop, lunch, same, science, sort

Answer Key *(cont.)*

Page 81

1. x 18 x 22 = 396 servings
2. – $25.00 – $12.93 = $12.07
3. ÷ 50 ÷ 10 = 5 coins
4. – 18 – 6 = 12 fish
5. ÷ 60 ÷ 10 = 6 hens
6. x 9 x 4 =36 people
7. + 30 + 7 = 37 cars
8. x 50 x 6 = 300 stars
9. ÷ 32 ÷ 4 = 8 paper clips
10. – 97° – 80° = 17°

Page 82

1. She climbed down her bedpost.
2. She was glad her mother did not see the mess under her bed.
3. She arranged the dollhouse furniture.
4. They ate her leftover cookies from her bedtime snack.
5. She actually found cookie crumbs in her dollhouse.

Page 83

1. D
2. A
3. B

Page 84

1. thousands
2. hundreds
3. tens
4. thousands
5. tens
6. hundreds
7. ones
8. thousands
9. thousands
10. hundreds
11. circle 8, tens
12. circle 4, hundreds
13. circle 7, thousands
14. circle 8, tens
15. circle 8, tens
16. circle 9, thousands
17. circle 7, thousands
18. circle 9, hundreds
19. circle 8, thousands
20. circle 8, tens
21. 5,210—1,025
22. 4,332—2,334
23. 7,630—3,067
24. 6,653—3,566
25. 7,522—2,257
26. 8,644—4,468
27. 5,421—1,245
28. 9,876—6,789

Page 85

1. tires, steering wheels, bumpers
2. refrigerators, ovens, frying pans
3. ears, knees, thumbs

Page 86

5 – Arkansas

6 – Columbia

1 – Mississippi

2 – Missouri

9 – Ohio

8 – Red

4 – Rio Grande

10 – St. Lawrence

7 – Snake

3 – Yukon

1. Mississippi
2. St. Lawrence
3. Arkansas
4. Snake
5. 4
6. 4
7. 2
8. 1,396 + 1,979 + 1,083 = 4,458 miles
9. 2,348 + 1,018 + 981 = 4,347 miles
10. 2,315 – 1,979 = 336 miles
11. 1,210 – 760 = 450 miles

Page 87

1. ! exclamatory
2. . declarative
3. ? interrogative
4. ? interrogative
5. . declarative
6. ! exclamatory or . imperative
7. ! exclamatory or . imperative
8. ! exclamatory or . declarative
9. ? interrogative
10. ! exclamatory or . imperative
11. ? interrogative
12. ! exclamatory or . declarative
13. ! exclamatory
14. . imperative
15. ? interrogative

Page 88

1. trees
2. boys' names
3. streets
4. cities
5. bugs or insects
6. books
7. feelings
8. countries
9. toys
10. clothes
11. oceans
12. shoes
13. vegetables
14. sandwiches
15. sports

Writing Paper

Writing Paper

Writing Paper

Writing Paper